EMS in Crime Scene

EMS in Crime Scene

Role of Medical Emergency Teams in Forensic Cases

Albino Manuel Gomes
Forensic Nurse Examiner - ANEFOR, Lisbon, Portugal

ELSEVIER
ACADEMIC PRESS
An imprint of Elsevier

Academic Press is an imprint of Elsevier
125 London Wall, London EC2Y 5AS, United Kingdom
525 B Street, Suite 1650, San Diego, CA 92101, United States
50 Hampshire Street, 5th Floor, Cambridge, MA 02139, United States
The Boulevard, Langford Lane, Kidlington, Oxford OX5 1GB, United Kingdom

British Library Cataloguing-in-Publication Data
A catalogue record for this book is available from the British Library

Library of Congress Cataloging-in-Publication Data
A catalog record for this book is available from the Library of Congress

ISBN: 978-0-12-824420-3

For Information on all Academic Press publications
visit our website at https://www.elsevier.com/books-and-journals

Publisher: Stacy Masucci
Acquisitions Editor: Elizabeth Brown
Editorial Project Manager: Mariana L. Kuhl
Production Project Manager: Maria Bernard
Cover Designer: Christian J. Bilbow

Typeset by MPS Limited, Chennai, India

CONTENTS

INTRODUCTION

This book aims to analyze the intervention of emergency medical teams at the crime scene, as well as their role in preserving evidences, in the context of violent death situations. Being a topic that has been little addressed, previous studies and documentation directed to the practice of these medical teams in the preservation of evidences are very scarce. However, its relevance is fundamental. The traces found in the places where violent death occurs can corroborate the police investigation or even lead investigators to different perspectives than those considered at the initial moment. Emergency medical teams are often the first to arrive on the scene, so their role in preserving evidences is particularly important.

As is well known, the priority of medical teams is to provide medical assistance to victims as well as to safeguard the interests of the family and society. However, the preservation of evidences must also constitute a relevant role for medical teams in the initial approach to the crime scene. This preservation of evidence extends to the hospital context, namely to the emergency services, where victims are often transported without direct intervention by out-of-hospital medical teams, who also present traces that will be important for the investigation. To obtain a conclusive result, arising from the examination of the place where the violent death occurred and the lifting of the corpse, it is very important to preserve and examine the area and the items related to the event (objects, stains, odors, brands).

The main objective of preserving a place where a crime occurred is, from the outset, to keep the environment as unchanged as possible, that is, not to move and/or subtract objects from their original position (even if it is a firearm) and not to add elements that were not present at the scene, such as shoe marks, dirt, hair strands, cigarette butts, and so on. However, it happens that the training program for emergency medical courses, given to doctors, paramedics, and nurses who work in the pre-hospital, does not include training on the elements that are relevant in the case of crime and, in particular, their identification and preservation.

The preservation of evidences, in the event of a crime, should be a subsidiary activity that does not compromise the victim's medical approach. In this way, this book intends to highlight the importance that medical teams can have in the preservation of evidences as well as in the registration of information inherent to the place where a crime occurred.

CHAPTER 1

Emergency and urgency: concepts and evolution

In this chapter, I will try to contextualize how the techniques for providing urgent and/or emerging care were developed, from the oldest civilizations in the world to the most recent times.

Evolution of urgent and/or emergent cares in prehospital environment

Since the beginning of his existence, man has been a victim of situations that unexpectedly alter his homeostatic system, whether in the psychological, biological, social, or cultural context. However, it is mainly from the psychobiological sphere that due to their nature and severity, they quickly need an external intervention without which their own existence will be in danger [1]. Indeed, in the oldest civilizations in the world, and for a long time, when an individual needed urgent and/or emergent care, the population redeemed itself from fatality and believed that only supernatural or spiritual intervention forces could save the victim from death [2].

However, already in the fourth century BCE, the father of Medicine, Hippocrates, stated that "Les moments favorables pour intervenir passent promptement et la mort survient si on a trop différé." Hippocrates and Galen, at this time, attempted to resuscitate their patients [2,3]. After a few centuries of little evolution, it was only at the beginning of the sixth century that some development began to take place. In Europe, after the great population movements, Emperor Mauricius created a group of knights responsible for "raising" the wounded in the fighting against the Barbarians, people existing at the time (Fontanella, Chavagnac) [2].

In the middle of the High Middle Ages, violent wars took place, some waged with the aim of spreading the Christian faith. With these

EMS in Crime Scene. DOI: https://doi.org/10.1016/B978-0-12-824420-3.00012-5

wars, it was necessary to develop appropriate organizational plans for battles that lasted several days, with the main objective of attending to the avalanche of wounded, sick, and dead. Thus for the provision of care, military nursing orders were created, based on religious principles, charity, and assistance to others, as well as hospitals for treating the wounded and needy [2].

In the 11th century, there are already testimonies that show the existence of "chevaliers infirmiers," who were trained by Greek and Arab doctors, so that they could help the wounded in the war camps, under tents that were installed on the slopes of the camps battle. Still in this century, a group of doctors, of which Avicene stands out, considered "Prince des Médecins," Arab philosophers and physicists traveled a series of battlefields and verified that the great part of the wounded had already been provided with the first care [2].

In the 14th century, in 1393, a real structure was created to provide emergency relief in Milan, Italy, because a monumental cathedral was being built, in which a large number of men worked (stone cutters, hand workers of among others) that needed a lot of care. This urgent care delivery structure remained active for around 150 years [2,4].

In the 16th century, there was an important milestone: the means to transport patients to the hospital are emerging. The Hospital de St. Jean de Bruges already had "ambulances chaises à porteurs" [2,4]. In the same century, there are records that André Vesale, in 1543, started the first tests of endotracheal intubation in animals, having also been responsible for controlled ventilation with intermittent positive pressure. A few years later, the definitive notion of an outpatient hospital was developed for the first time in order to help the sick and war-wounded. At the end of this century, military ambulances were created by Sully, who, at the time of the siege of the Amiens, in France, were in charge of lifting and transporting the survivors after the combat [2,4].

In the 17th century, there was an important advance in the study of the human body, in Universities such as Bologna, Italy, where cadavers were dissected, which led to a better understanding of the physiology and anatomy of the human body. In 1616 William Harvey described blood circulation and cardiac functioning. In parallel, Hooke presented, in 1667, a ventilation technique that consisted of insufflation of exhaled air, into the lungs, with the aid of a tube placed in the trachea [2,5].

The middle of the 18th century (approximately) marks the end of resignation to ancestral ideas, in the face of accidental death. Thus man seeks to explain the causes that lead to death, through scientific investigation and thus interrupts the evolution of the notion of fatality. New ideas, new conceptions of care emerge, and above all, man comes to have a part of his destiny [2].

In 1708 a law was created in France that created a health service in armies. These would be present at the battle scenes and had, from the outset, doctors, and surgeons to care for the wounded, as well as nurses who had become irreplaceable in the tents and aid posts of the battle fronts. The wounded soldiers were thus removed from the battle scenes to the rear, and subsequently assisted there. Literature points out that, at the end of this century, Baron Dominick Jean Larrey, chief physician of Napoleon Bonaparte, recognized the importance of immediate prehospital care, having created the "Flying Ambulance" to remove the wounded from the battlefield and introduced the norm that those who work in this ambulance should be properly trained to provide medical care during transportation.

According to some authors, these are the first historical reports that document what could be the beginning of a medical emergency system. Thus the simple idea of transporting victims from the place where the situation occurred to a place where they could be assessed and assisted [2,6,7] arose. Since 1732, the Scottish doctor Tossack has been practicing the first mouth-to-mouth resuscitations in adults, only in 1744 and he would see the success of his resuscitation practices. In 1740 the concept of "medical emergency" was formally born, written by R.A. Ferchault Réaumur, by order of Louis XV, and later posted on the walls throughout the Kingdom of France. In this same text, the author describes the various methods of resuscitation known at the time and commits the people in general to practice them with perseverance. It is also recognized that aid, to be effective, requires speed [1,2].

During the 19th century, studies and discoveries emerged that increasingly contributed to the better success and recovery of a life in imminent danger. Florence Nightingale, for example, was notable for the good services she provided in the relief and care of the wounded during the Crimean War (1854–55). In 1858 Silvester proposes his techniques of artificial ventilation and cardiac massage, represented in the figure. These techniques were widely used until the first half of the following century [2].

In 1866 a precise definition of the concept of ambulance appears, as a temporary hospital, located a short distance from the population and the arms divisions, with the aim of accompanying movements and ensuring first aid to the wounded and other sick. In 1892 Maass successfully demonstrated external cardiorespiratory resuscitation in patients [2,8].

Although the first attempts at resuscitation were at a remarkable stage of development until the beginning of the 20th century, these were mostly unsuccessful, since there was no scientific demonstration of the effectiveness of all the technical steps to be carried out on the ground, since there is no communication and collaboration between the researchers and the teams that provided direct care on the spot. At the same time, there were no effective action protocols, with their continued application at the site of the event, during transport and at the hospital itself [9]. Thus it was in the first half of the 20th century that the main advances in the field of emergency medicine, in the field of telecommunications and transport, developed, to which war conflicts continued to be the major contributors [2,7].

A brief notion of the definitive trauma treatment times in the different wars allows us to analyze how much the time factor has been of real importance in guaranteeing a low morbidity and mortality of the victims. Thus in World War I, it took an average of 12–18 hours of time to treat a trauma, with a mortality rate of 8.5%. Later, in the Vietnam War, the trauma treatment time was only 65 minutes, with a considerably lower mortality rate of 1.7% [6].

During the Korean War conflicts in the 1950s and the Vietnam War in the 1960s and 1970s, substantial advances were made in the field of trauma care, as well as in the improvement and discovery of new resuscitation techniques. The vast majority of resuscitations were initiated on the scene, by experienced teams and with adequate equipment, as happened during the great World Wars, in which many nurses were enlisted in the military [7].

During the last half of the 20th century, however, there was a significant increase in the rate of morbidity and mortality in civil society, due to the progressive change in the field of accidents, in view of the imminent industrial and technological advance, both in industrialized countries, or in others in development. Given this reality, initiatives for the prevention of traffic accidents and aid organizations for victims have been created. The latter, while acting downstream, prevent and avoid many of the disastrous consequences. In this way, all the experience acquired during wartime is transferred to civil society, from rescue techniques (in order to reduce the rate of morbidity and mortality for victims) to the organized way of responding to prehospital emergency situations. in relation to detection, alert, prehelp, help, assisted transport, and assistance in the health unit.

This was the basic philosophy of a medical emergency system that, over time, was created and that several countries in the world adopt, adapting it to their needs and developing it in the best possible way, according to their resources and local realities [1,2].

CHAPTER 2

Criminal investigation historical aspects

I would like to begin this chapter with a phrase uttered exactly 100 years ago: "Investigation is, should be, an exact science and, as such, treated coldly, without the slightest emotion." This statement was produced at a particularly important moment in the creation of a new attitude toward the judicial evidence. In fact, after the intellectual rebellion—and sometimes with strong social resonance—of the 18th century Enlightenment thinkers, with particular emphasis on Voltaire and Rousseau, against the decisions of the judges who systematically fell into judicial error—the criminal investigation was the object of attention by an important body of scholars and scientists who increasingly sought to adjust penalties to the nature of criminal responsibility.

Consolidated the confidence in the power of scientific knowledge, modeled, among others, by positivism and the method of natural sciences, the concern started to be the creation of systems that explain the apprehended phenomena, through the establishment of laws. In this way, science became synonymous with absolute knowledge, with an unquestionable capture of the real without recourse to philosophy and, particularly, metaphysics. It was under the effects of this ideological organization of the sciences that men like Locard, Lacassagne[1], Lombroso[2], among many,

[1] Lacassagne—Alexandre Lacassagne dedicated his life to the study, teaching, and the advancement of forensic science. He worked for decades as a professor at the University of Lyon in France, participated in numerous forensic investigations, and served as a consultant and expert in many criminal trials. Lacassagne is also known as one of the first people to conduct analysis of blood stain patterns and was the first scientist to study bullet marks and their relationship to specific weapons.

[2] Lombroso—Cesare Lombroso was an Italian doctor and psychiatrist. His work on crime laid the foundation for modern criminology. He moved away from the nature of crime in relation to the criminal's motivations and habits. Lombroso was interested in studying the physical differences between the different parts of the Italian population. In 1862 he began anthropometric measurements of 3000 soldiers and was also interested in psychiatry and criminal anthropology. His 1876 book Criminal Man argues that some people were born criminals—they claimed that they were "atavistic," or that they were set back to a primitive stage of evolution. Lombroso believed that "primitiveness" could be read from the bodies and habits of criminals—for example, facial features, body type, and tattoos, which he saw as a particular sign of criminality. Lombroso's emphasis on external brands and "primitiveness" was part of a broader movement in the late 19th century. This movement believed that biology and inheritance explained human behavior.

EMS in Crime Scene. DOI: https://doi.org/10.1016/B978-0-12-824420-3.00004-6

advanced to a sociological, medical, and anthropological research on the causes of crime, according to deterministic logic. Thus the approach to the object of study had, in the first line of concerns, studying the crime, the criminal, and the relationships that were established between the in the first line of concerns, to study the crime, the criminal, and the relations that were established between the act and the subject of the illegal conduct, in order to quantify the degree of guilt and responsibility, which are the fundamental criteria for the application of the condemnatory penalties.

The criminal investigation, emerging from 1890, privileged at first the relationship between the act and the subject, leaving crime in the sphere of sociological interest and the criminal under the attention of anthropologists and alienists. Based on laboratory experimentalism or ontological techniques, the new scientists tried to generate a type of evidence that, due to its scientific nature, would guarantee the impossibility of judicial error and remove the evidence par excellence in force in the old regime at the process level, the defendant's confession. It is no wonder, therefore, that the subjects with the most empirical approach were chosen to create, at the state level, what was designated by the scientific police—chemistry, physics (with particular emphasis on dynamics and ballistics), biology, medicine, thanatology, fingerprinting, anatomy, among others.

These sciences contributed to an interdisciplinary practice, based on the analysis and formulation of material evidence, starting from a principle defined by the aforementioned Edmond Locar[3] and which has gone down in history with the designation of "Locard principle or exchange," according to which: "at the crime scene, there are necessarily traces of the criminal who, in turn, carries with him, voluntarily or involuntarily, traces of the place where he committed the criminal action" [10].

This formulation structurally changed the attitude toward the construction of the criminal process: the new criminal investigator, armed with scientific reason, turned to the crime scene, and looked for the

[3] Edmond Locard—He was a pioneer of Forensic Science, also known as the Sherlock Holmes of France. He formulated the basic principle of forensic science: "Every contact leaves a mark," which became known as the Locard Exchange Principle. Like all principles, it is based on a simple idea, but of great depth. Locard studied medicine and law in Lyon, becoming Alexandre Lacassagne's assistant, criminologist and professor. In 1910 he started to found his own criminal laboratory. He produced a monumental seven-volume work, Traité de Criminalistique, and, in 1918 described twelve characteristic points for the identification of fingerprints.

footprint, the hair, the drop of blood, the fingerprints, looking at the corpse not only as if it were a body without a soul, but an operative object, all to the detriment of testimonies, confrontations, and confessions. Through the vestiges, it was possible to see if the individual had been strangled, showed signs of struggle, if it had been suicide, if it had been homicide camouflaged by a false suicide, if he had been injured, what type of cadaveric books, body position, and the calculation of time of death using cadaveric rigidity [11].

The autopsy bench and the laboratory bench started to consolidate (or not) the hypotheses examined at the crime scene, and from them, the relations were established between criminal and crime. Thus the fingerprint of the individual who was on desk y of individual x. And despite the fact that he denied that he had ever entered that office, the fingerprint collected was more true than the testimony of individual A. The hair collected on the corpse's nails they belonged to individual A. The bullet found in the body of individual B could only have been fired by the weapon seized from individual F, and so on.

In fact, the judicial system has always been extremely conservative in relation to the vanguard of these advanced spectators, who constituted the scientific police laboratories and the institutes of forensic medicine. However, from then on, fiction never abandoned the police, following the evolution of scientific determinism.

Sherlock Holmes'[4] method was based on three basic principles—observation, deduction, and knowledge:

- Observation: His obsession with paying attention to details at the crime scene was startling, due to his peculiar habits.
- Deduction: "It is of the utmost importance, in the art of deduction, to know how to distinguish, among the various facts, which are of vital importance," he guarantees. According to Watson, at the scene of the crime, "Holmes took a tape measure and a round lens from his pocket. Armed with these two instruments, he began to walk quickly and silently around the room, sometimes stopping, sometimes kneeling and, at certain moments, stretching the entire

[4] Sherlock Holmes—He is a fictional character in British literature created by the doctor and writer Sir Arthur Conan Doyle. Holmes is a researcher from the late 19th century, early 20th century. His first appearance was in 1887 in the magazine Beeton's Christmas Annual, in the story "A Study in Red."

length on the floor." The observer's ability to remain logical and entirely objective is of paramount importance in deductive analysis. Knowing how to approach the case with a completely clear mind is always an advantage. In fact, it is a mistake to conclude the analysis of the data early, because it ends up distorting them to fit our theories.

- Knowledge: About his own knowledge, he wrote, in 1926, in the text "The lion's mane": "I have a vast collection of unusual knowledge, which do not follow scientific norms, but which are very useful for the purposes of my work." Holmes' statement in the text is better understood now: the mystery of the boscombe[5] valley: "you know my method, it is based on observing the little things. the apparently most insignificant things are the most important."

In fact, it is this accumulated knowledge that often provides the final element for completing a criminal investigation, but not only. In fact, it also confirms the confidence that the flesh and blood policemen are capable of achieving the ideal of justice that lives within each one of us.

Thanatology[6] had asserted itself since 1899, anatomopathology was becoming more consistent, and microbiology was taking its first steps. This whole web of knowledge was intended to serve the criminal investigation, to provide it with laboratory instrumentation that would deliver to the judicial evidence a value of truth so solid that its understanding in the light of the deductive method would place on the secondary level both the confession and the value of the testimony.

Locard would even proclaim the new scientific police, which then emerged as the main brake against the practice of torture, since any confession by the defendant was necessary to prove a crime.

[5] Mystery of the boscombe valley—This is one of the 56 short stories of Sherlock Holmes written by Sir Arthur Conan Doyle, being the fourth of 12 stories in The Adventures of Sherlock Holmes. It was first published in Strand Magazine in 1891.

[6] Thanatology—It is the scientific study of death. Thanatology investigates the forensic mechanisms and aspects of death, such as the bodily changes that accompany the period after death, as well as the broader social and legal aspects. It is mainly an interdisciplinary study. The word is derived from Thanatos (in Greek "death"), god of Greek mythology that personified death, plus the suffix logia, which derives from the Greek legein ("to speak") and means study. In 1901 Elie Metchnikoff, who received the Nobel Prize for Medicine in 1908, coined the term "Thanatology," calling it the science responsible for death. At that time, Thanatology was considered a branch of forensic medicine.

Since then, generations of scientists and technicians have dedicated their lives to integrating more knowledge in the search for evidence, commonly known as material evidence, destroying the forms of criminal proceedings based on testimony and confession, which transformed European courts during the nineteenth century, in the largest gallery of horrors and injustice that there is memory.

Disciplines such as fingerprinting, forensic photography, biochemistry, and physics began to assert themselves from then on as indispensable for the construction of criminal evidence. Its technical-scientific apparatus was recognized by the state as important in the field of court action.

CHAPTER 3

Physiopathology of death

Because it is fundamental to understanding the general theme of this book, a smooth approach to the death process is carried out. The biological concept says that life is a set of structured and organized processes that are in balance. In this biological concept, death is a set of pathophysiological processes that tend toward irreversibility. Because it is a process, not something that occurs at a certain moment, it has several periods.

Death is the cessation of the function of three systems: cardiovascular system, respiratory system, and central venous system[1].

Death process

The death process consists essentially of four periods:

1. Agonic period—Period of time when the pathophysiological, irreversible processes of vital functions begin and develop; cells no longer functioning or have metabolic activities or aerobic respiration. Different tissues die at a different rate; the cerebral cortex tolerates only few minutes of anoxia, whereas connective tissue and muscles may survive longer (for hours).
2. Period of somatic or relative death—Period of time when vital functions irreversibly cease, when death occurs and when legal personality ceases. There is an effective suspension of nervous, circulatory, and respiratory functions; the person is irreversibly unconscious, not aware of the surrounding environment and is unable to appreciate sensory stimuli or initiate any voluntary movement. Reflex nervous activity may persist, and circulatory and respiratory function continue either spontaneously or with artificial support. Somatic

[1] Indications of death: Unconsciousness; loss of all reflexes; no reaction to painful stimuli; muscular flaccidity; cessation of heart rate and respiratory movement; eye signs: loss of corneal and light reflexes; mid-dilated position of the pupils; irregular size and shape of the pupils; eyelids usually closed incompletely. Tache noire: where the sclera remains exposed, two triangles of discoloration appear at each side of the cornea, either brown or black.

EMS in Crime Scene. DOI: https://doi.org/10.1016/B978-0-12-824420-3.00002-2

death = brain death = vegetative state (all tissue and cells of the body are alive and functioning except for those damaged in the central nervous system).
3. Intermediate death period—Period of time in which the changes following the cessation of vital functions (cardiovascular and respiratory) appear. In the first stage, abiotic phenomena occur and then proliferative destruction.
4. Period of absolute death—Period of time when biological activity ceases and there is a total absence of manifestation of cellular and biological life, leaving the corpse reduced to a simple inert organic heap.

In the period of intermediate death, the so-called positive signs of death appear, which, in turn, are divided into early and late signs. The early signs are body temperature, cadaveric dehydration, livor mortis, and rigor mortis (RM). The late signs are autolysis and putrefaction.

Medicolegal importance of death diagnosis:

- detect cause of death
- manner of death
- know time of death
- social reasons
- organ donation
- apparent death
- statistical reasons
- heritage reasons

Early signs of death

Body temperature/body cooling/algor mortis

Early signs of death consist of decreasing temperature of the body until it equals the ambient temperature. This is a physical phenomenon of heat loss. There are several factors that influence body temperature – constitutional factors, environmental factors, and the cause of death [12].

It is the most useful indicator of time of death during the first 24 hours postmortem.

After death, all metabolic activity ceases rapidly (muscles, liver) and circulation stops, heat production ceases soon after death. The body surface begins cooling immediately after death, followed by a delay in deep organs cooling, until a heat gradient is set up between the core of the body and the surface. In practice, the temperature is either measured per rectum or intrahepatic via an abdominal stab.

The rate of body cooling:

- 1°C/hour in summer
- 1.5°C/hour in winter

Factors that influence body temperature
Constitutional/individual (age, stature; state of nutrition; clothing)
Environmental (temperature, environment, humidity)
Cause of death (faster in bleeding, alcohol intoxication, and chronic disease; slower in nicotine intoxication and infectious disease)
Obese—cooling speed is slower
Fetus—cooling speed is greater

Determination of the time of death by body temperature usually involves using a formula: time since death = 37°C – rectal temperature (c) + 3

If the team decides to take rectal temperature, the rectum must always be examined prior to the insertion of the thermometer.

Cadaveric dehydration

Consists of evaporation, in a ventilated, dry, and high-temperature environment. It occurs in areas of thin epidermis, exposed to the air or chafed, manifested by:

- skin tightening (yellow-amber color and hard consistency)
- dehydration of the mucous membranes (which acquire a dark brown color)
- alterations at the eye level (when the eyelids are not closed properly, due to opacities of the cornea, spots in the sclera, or sinking of the eyeball)

Corneal opacification can occur between 45 minutes and 4 hours after death [13]. Sinking of the eyeball can also occur due to the evaporation of water from the eyes. In newborns, this phenomenon is more visible, giving general phenomena such as weight loss. These phenomena are classified as "artifacts of death," and they can sometimes lead to misinterpretations of ill-treatment.

Livor mortis/hypostasis

After death occurs, circulation of blood ceases and subsequent movement of blood is by gravity. Blood accumulates in the capillaries in the dependent parts of the body (purple or reddish-purple discoloration of the adjacent skin). In pressure areas such as the shoulder blades, buttock, and calves, discoloration will be pale. It starts immediately after death. Apparent after 2 hours and fixed after 8 hours. May not appear at all especially in infants, old people, and anemic people [13].

As a general rule, the discolorations are purple in color[2], but they can present with

- bright red or carmine color (carbon monoxide poisoning)
- dark vinous color (death by asphyxiation)
- pink color (death from bleeding, hypothermia, and some drowning)
- purplish-green color (putrefaction started).

Early hours after death it appears in the form of blotchy postmortem hypostasis, which usually sinks down and becomes confluent on the most dependant area. Once hypostasis is established, there is controversy about its ability to undergo subsequent gravitational shift if the body is moved into a different posture.

Primary hypostasis may either

- remain fixed
- move completely to the newly dependant zone
- be partly fixed and partly relocated

The color, extent, and distribution of the bloodstains are important, as they indicate the position in which the body remained. Livor mortis is not very important in determining the time of death. It is important in determining whether the body has been moved.

Sites of hypostasis:

Depends on the position of the body before death:

[2] Color of hypostasis: The color of hypostasis is variable and depends on the state of oxygenation at death. Usual color is blue-pink. It is a crude indicator of the mode of death. cherry-pink: CO poisoning; dark blue-pink: cyanide poisoning; brown: methahemoglobinemia; bronze: septic abortion caused by *Clostridium perfringes*; pallor: anemia, hemorrhage (or normal in extremes of age).

- Supine:
  - shoulders, buttocks
  - heels pressing against the surface give white color (pale)
- Vertical (hanging):
  - distally in legs and feet
- Drowning:
  - chest, upper chest, and upper limbs
- Face-down death:
  - as in *epilepsy, drunken victims*
  - whitening around the nose and lips
- Hypostasis may also occur in viscera
- Heart: mistaken for myocardial infarction (MI)
- Lungs: mistaken for pneumonia
- Intestine: mistaken for hemorrhagic infarction

Timing and permanence of hypostasis: Hypostasis appears at variable times after death. May appear half an hour to many hours after death. In the early hours after death, it appears in the form of blotchy postmortem hypostasis which usually sinks down and becomes confluent on the most dependent area.

Hypostasis	Bruises
Dependent areas	Anywhere
Well defined edges	Ill-defined edges
Blood is retained in intact capillaries	Blood escapes through ruptured capillaries
Superficial	Deep into skin
Same level on surface	Raised
Pale over pressure areas	Red
Incision: blood flows from the cut vessel (washable)	Incision: blood coagulates in tissue
No swelling	May be with swelling

Medicolegal importance of hypostasis:

- sign of death
- cause of death
- time estimation
- position before/after death
- indicate if the body was moved or not after death

Rigor mortis

Consists of the contraction of the entire musculature, which appears after death and occurs after the first period of primary flaccidity (beginning 2 hours after death, being complete at 12 hours and maximum at 24 hours) [13].

One of the recognizable signs of death is a chemical change in the muscles after death, causing the limbs of the corpse to become stiff and difficult to move or manipulate.

Unlike normal muscle contractions, the body is unable to complete the cycle and release the coupling between the myosin and actin, creating a perpetual state of muscular contraction, until the breakdown of muscle tissue by digestive enzymes during decomposition.

RM is initiated when the ATP concentration falls to 85% of normal.

Sequence:

- primary muscular flaccidity
- generalized muscular stiffness
- secondary muscular flaccidity

RM starts to develop about 2–3 hours after death. Usually, it is first detected in smaller muscle groups such as those around the eyes, mouth, jaw and fingers. It resolves in the same order in which it develops. It concludes around 36–48 hours after death. RM usually disappears with decomposition.

Factors affecting timing of RM:

- *Environmental temperature:*
  - cold and wet → onset slow, duration longer
  - hot and dry → onset fast, duration shorter
- *Muscular activity before death:*
  - muscles healthy and robust, at rest before death → slow onset, duration longer;
  - muscles exhausted/fatigued → onset rapid, especial in those limbs being used (e.g., in someone running at the time of death, lower limbs develop RM faster than upper limbs);
  - increase activity (convulsions, electrocution, lightning) → rapid onset and short duration.
- *Age:*
  - extremes of age → rapid onset.

- *Cause of death:*
  - asphyxia, pneumonia, nervous disease with muscle paralysis and dehydration → slow onset;
  - septicemia and poisoning → rapid onset, may even be absent, especial in limbs affected by septicemia;
  - emaciated or died of wasting disease → rapid onset, short duration.

Medicolegal importance of RM:

- time estimation
- cause of death
- know position
- sign of death

Cadaveric spasm

It is muscle contraction without primary flaccidity. It is a phenomenon that can fix the victim's attitude at the time of death. It is relatively rare; however, it is observable in localized muscle groups, namely in the hands, in cases of violent death [13]. Also known as instantaneous rigor, cataleptic rigidity, or instantaneous rigidity. Rare form of muscular stiffening that occurs at the moment of death persists into the period of RM and can be mistaken for RM. The cause is unknown but usually associated with violent deaths happening with intense emotion.

May affect all muscles in the body, but typically only groups, such as the forearms, or hands seen in cases of drowning victims when grass, weeds, roots, or other materials are clutched and provides proof of life at the time of entry into the water. Often demonstrates the last activity one did prior to death and is therefore significant in forensic investigations, for example, clinging on a knife tightly.

On the scene, a first determination of the date of death can be made, analyzing the temperature of the body (rectal, axillary), the ambient temperature, the rigidity, and the cadaveric livors. The determination of the temperature of the scene must be done in an area close to the body, pointing out all the existing factors that may have delayed or accelerated the process of cadaveric cooling (clothes, air conditioning, heaters, fireplaces, etc.).

Among the new techniques that promise greater precision in the determination of postmortem interval (IPM)[3] are fluorescence spectroscopy of cadaver skin, histological modifications, especially bone marrow, determination of nitrogen, amino acid, and citrate levels and reaction of bone tissue with luminol.

Decomposition

Decomposition involves two processes: autolysis and putrefaction. Autolysis is the breakdown of cells and organs through an aseptic chemical process caused by intracellular enzymes. Putrefaction is due to bacteria and fermentation. Putrefaction depends on two main factors: the environment and the body. Decomposition can be divided into putrefaction, mummification, adipocere, and skeletonization.

Putrefaction

The normal final sign of death starts immediately after death at the cellular level. Becomes visible in 48–72 hours. Its onset may be sped up or delayed by several factors mainly: temperature and humidity[4].

Influences on putrefaction: A high environmental humidity will enhance putrefaction. The rate of putrefaction is influenced by the bodily habits of the decedent; obese individuals putrefy more rapidly than those who are lean. Putrefaction will be delayed in deaths from exsanguination (bleeding to death) because blood provides a channel for the spread of putrefactive organisms within the body. Conversely, putrefaction is more rapid in persons dying with widespread infection, congestive cardiac failure, or retention of sodium and salts. It tends to be more rapid in children than in adults, but the onset is relatively slow in unfed new-born infants because of the lack of commensal bacteria.

[3] IPM (postmortem interval): corresponds to the period of time between the occurrence of death and the moment when the body is found. Determining the date of death is one of the essential components in the course of a forensic investigation; however, it is still an underdeveloped area, as there are few tests to determine this value and even these are sometimes easily fallible. This dating is not always easy to do, as it is too dependent on several factors. Superficially, it is related to the analysis of the body's natural cadaverous phenomena, but as these too are not very objective and vary depending on the influence of internal and external factors, which results from this analysis, the probable date of the event is often an approximate value or up to a time interval.

[4] Two phenomena for putrefaction: Autolysis: occurs by digestive enzymes released from the cells after death. Bacterial action: most of them come from the bowel and *Clostridium welchii* predominates (same bacteria that causes gas gangrene)

Heavy clothing and other coverings, by retaining body heat, will speed up putrefaction. Rapid putrefactive changes may be seen in corpses left in a room which is well heated, or in a bed with an electric blanket.

Injuries to the body surface promote putrefaction by providing portals of entry for bacteria and the associated blood provides an excellent medium for bacterial growth.

Death certificate

The death certificate[5] must be completed according to the WHO guidelines. In Part I of the document, each of the items corresponds to one of the "causes of death":

1. Direct cause—illness or injury that directly caused the death (excludes death mechanisms such as cardiorespiratory arrest).
2. Intermediate cause—disease that constitutes an antecedent condition directly or indirectly related to the direct cause of death or external agent that produced the fatal injuries.
3. Basic cause—disease that started the chain of pathological events or circumstances of the accident or violence that produced the injury.
4. Original cause—what is at the origin or triggered the causes of paragraphs (1), (2) and (3).

[5] Death certificate: The death certificate identifies the corpse, attests to the fact and must indicate the cause of death. The study of the causes of death allows epidemiological knowledge of the populations; monitoring trends and patterns of disease; establishment of guidelines for health promotion, allocation of resources, planning of services, definition of priorities in health policy. Data are recorded centrally, and coding is based on the *International Classification of Diseases* (*ICD 10*) of the World Health Organization (WHO), on a regular basis and with previously defined criteria, so that these statistics can be compared regionally, national and international.

CHAPTER 4

Violent death

According to Genovial França [14], violent death is understood to be the result of, directly or indirectly, the action of external agents: "It is death resulting from an exogenous and harmful action, or that such action has contributed to aggravate an already existing pathology, as long as there is a cause-effect correlation between the action and death; Violent death is also understood as one in which there is no violence in the physical sense of the word, but whose neglect (failure to help, for example), was the cause of death."

Depending on the circumstances in which violent death occurs, it can be classified as accidental, suicidal, and homicidal, all of which imply different legal consequences. Among these implications will be, for example, the calculation of compensation or pension to beneficiaries, the payment or not of insurance premiums, and the establishment of a cause–effect link between the violence committed by the aggressor and death [15].

External agents

External agents are constituted by a source of physical energy, or external chemical, capable of producing, in the human body, anatomical and/or functional injuries (traumatic injuries). They can be divided into mechanical agents, physical agents, chemical agents, and toxic agents [16].

External mechanical agents

Mechanical agents are classified as follows:

- blunt instruments
- sharp instruments

EMS in Crime Scene. DOI: https://doi.org/10.1016/B978-0-12-824420-3.00010-1

- pointed instruments
- perforating instruments
- sharp-edged instruments
- blunt penetrating instruments

Blunt injuries

There are two distinct categories of wounds. The first category is blunt injuries. These wounds are caused by the crushing impact of a blunt object (baseball bat, interior of a car, or a fist) or when a moving person comes into contact with a stationary blunt object such as a wall or a tree. Blunt actions are caused when obtuse protrusions or hard surfaces touch with violence the human body. Blunt forces create contusions, bite marks, abrasions[1], bruises, ecchymosis[2], lacerations, ligature/restraint injuries, and fractures[3].

Falls from a considerable height, or when collapsing, being run over, or impacting vehicles, are examples of situations, which can also produce blunt injuries [16].

[1] Abrasion: abrasion is the lesions of the epidermis or dermis with formation of hematic crust. In the dead, there is no crusting. One of the most typical features of excoriation is its crust, which can have three different origins: serous, due to the lymph spillage from the injured vessels and as such it will have a yellow color; sero-hematic, in this case, there is a mixture of lymph and blood, when the dermal papillae are reached, which indicates a slightly deeper abrasion, and the crust will have a yellowish-red color; and hematic, when the crust is predominantly formed by blood, acquiring a dark reddish color. An excoriation typically occurs when the skin enters and contacts an opposite surface, with friction between them, which causes the surface layers of the skin to be pulled out. From a clinical point of view, it may not have much meaning, but for a medicolegal expert excoriation can be valuable, because, unlike bruises, excoriations accurately indicate the impact site of the blunt action.

[2] Ecchymosis: ecchymosis is a hemorrhagic infiltration in the tissue meshes, and for it to occur, it is necessary to have a more resistant plane, below the traumatized region, thus allowing blood to leak. Calabuig divides ecchymosis into several categories, according to the intensity of the contusion and the consequent blood spillage. As such, we can find bruises, in which the blood infiltrates the tissues in laminar form; ecchymomas, "as a synonym for ecchymosis of great proportion, an expression that is seldom used among us"; sugilations, which arise through suction (the characteristic "hickeys"); petechiae—small bruises, "almost always grouped and characterized by a hemorrhagic stipple," very present in death by asphyxiation, presenting at the level of the face and conjunctiva. The shape of bruises means a lot to coroners. Sometimes, he faithfully prints the mark of the objects that gave rise to him (figurative bruises).

[3] Fractures: Fractures result from the mechanisms of compression, flexion, or torsion and are characterized by the solution of continuity of the bones. They are called direct, when they occur at the trauma site, and indirect, when they arise from violence in a region more or less distant from the fractured site.

The second category is sharp injuries. These are wounds caused by an object that has a sharp edge (knife, saw, glass shard). As you will see, sharp injuries typically have clean-cut edges. Because of the nature of sharp injuries, they can cause extensive tissue destruction and internal organ damage.

Although each of these categories has specific characteristics, there are some common characteristics. In general, blunt injury is caused by an external force applying significant pressure to some area of your patient. The pressure causes injuries that range from bruises all the way to fractures. Blunt injuries can sometimes tell you the direction force was applied and even give you a pattern of the tool or weapon that caused the injury.

Contusion

A contusion, commonly referred to as a bruise, is one of the more common forms of blunt force trauma. A bruise results in blood leaking from capillaries under the surface of the skin. In general, a bruise will go from an initial purple-blue color to a greenish-yellow color. It is almost impossible to date a bruise to the exact time it occurred. However, if you see bruises ranging in appearance from fresh to old, your index of suspicion should be high. Sometimes you can give an approximate age to a bruise if other features, like a fracture or abrasion, are present.

Significant blunt forces do not necessarily produce bruising. The capillaries that burst from the resultant pressure may be below the epidermal layer or tissues subject to repeated trauma may scar, making it harder for blood to extravasate. Also, bruises may not be visible for hours, or even days. Today's forensic scientists have special instruments that use alternate light sources (infrared) to detect occult bruising. This technique is helpful in locating deep bruises that cannot be readily seen in the initial hours postinjury.

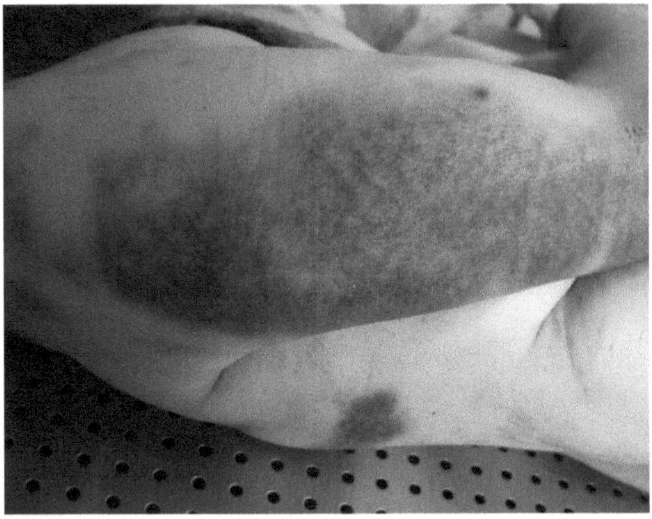

Picture 1—contusion.

Bruises

Bruises can be masked by the natural coloration of the skin. They can also be easily overlooked in areas into which blood has been forced or compressed into a confined space (application of a tourniquet or ligature) or when it has settled in dependent areas where circulation is failing. In elderly patients, it is important to consider this point. Bruising is caused when an impact damages blood vessels such that the blood leaks into the perivascular tissues and is evident on the skin surface as discoloration.

Generally, it is easier for blood to escape into looser tissue so bruising tends to be more common in certain body areas, among the frail or elderly population, and in cases of morbid obesity. Some people bruise easier than others and in cases of certain medical conditions or the effects of medications that change blood-clotting mechanisms (e.g., blood thinners), bruising may readily occur, even without trauma. Other factors that may make bruising more or less prominent are heat and cold and medications or physical conditions that affect vasodilation or vasoconstriction of superficial blood vessels. Most importantly, if a bruise fades in several days before the estimated time without significant color change, everything else must be questioned.

Initial color of the bruise is the product of natural skin pigment, the color of the pigment in the extravasated blood, and any color added by the inflammatory reaction. Such discoloration changes in color, shape, and location as the blood pigment is broken down and resorbed. In some cases, although the blood vessel may be damaged, there may be no visible evidence on the skin. In certain cases, it may take hours or days for a bruise to become apparent (as the blood diffuses through damaged tissue).

The site of the bruise does not necessarily indicate the site of impact as gravity, and other factors such as the presence or absence of tissue planes will allow blood to track to sites remote from the initial impact.

Types and patterns:

1. Finger bruises: consisting of circular or oval bruises from squeezing, poking, gripping, or grabbing injuries.
2. Linear petechial bruises: in the shape of a hand caused by capillary rupturing at the edge of the injury from high-velocity impact of the hand slap.
3. Pinch marks: consisting of paired, crescent-shaped bruises separated by a white line.
4. Coarse speckled (intradermal) bruises: from impact injuries through clothing. They lie just beneath the epidermis in the corium and are well defined.
5. Petechial bruises: pinprick bruises from ruptured capillaries, for example, suction bruises, squeezing, slapping, strangulation, and suffocation.

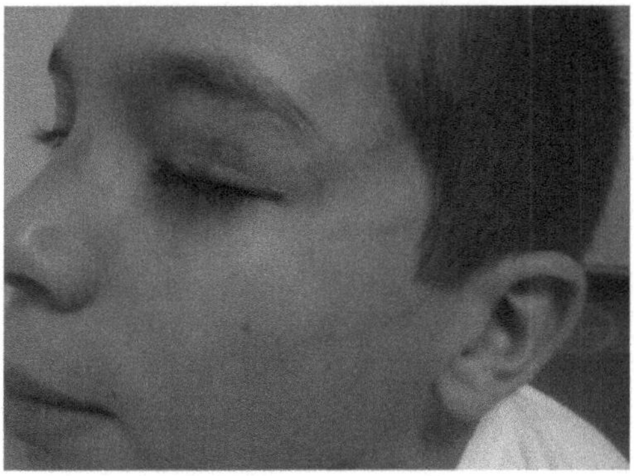

Picture 2—finger marks in face.

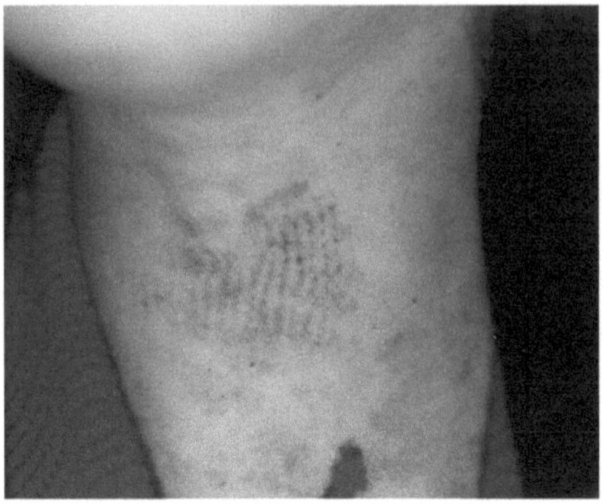

Picture 3—strangulation marks in neck.

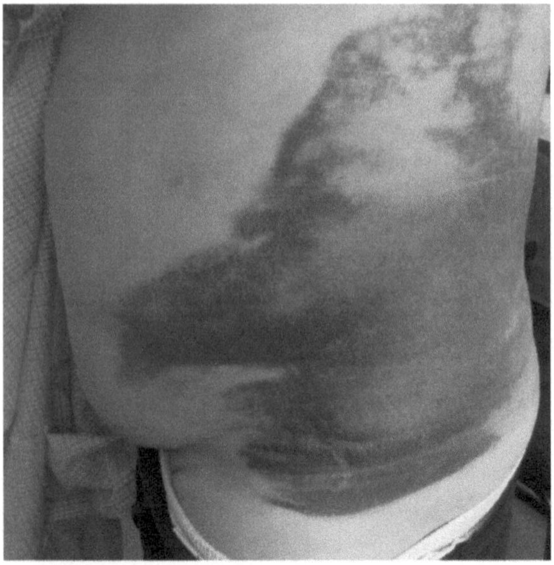

Picture 4—contusion with some days.

Sites more commonly associated with nonaccidental injury:

- facial: soft tissues of the cheek, eye, mouth, ear, mastoid, lower jaw, frenulum, and neck
- chest wall
- abdomen
- inner thighs and genitalia strongly associated with *sexual abuse*

- buttocks and outer thighs commonly associated with *punishment* injury
- multiple sites

Differential diagnosis of bruising:

1. accidental injury: commonly on bony surfaces;
2. artifact: dirt, paint, felt tip, dye from clothing or footwear;
3. benign tumors: halo nevus, blue nevus, hemangiomas;
4. vascular and bleeding disorders: thrombocytopenic purpura, hemophilia, purpura in association with infection, for example, meningococcal septicemia;
5. disturbances of pigmentation: café-au-lait patches, Mongolian blue spots;
6. erythematous lesions: erythema nodosum;
7. hereditary collagen disorders: osteogenesis imperfecta, Ehlers–Danlos syndrome.

Medicolegal importance: age of injury; degree of violence; different colors in the same victim are important, especially in child abuse.

Abrasion

Abrasions indicate contact with a rough surface or object. They also indicate the exact site of contact or impact. In living tissues, they will eventually become crust-like or form a scab. An abrasion is formed by the surface tissues being pushed forward toward one end of a sliding abrasion. They may exhibit characteristic patterns (i.e., motorcycle drive chains). This helps you because you can determine if the story matches the wounds. Also, in this type of wound, you can determine the point of impact (the bottom of the v-shape wound points in the direction of contact).

From a medicolegal point of view, the importance of abrasions results from the fact that they can provide information of great forensic relevance, namely the circumstances surrounding the facts. For example, the existence of abrasions around the mouth and nose can suggest a situation of suffocation, its location on the inner side of the thighs and around the genitals can indicate possible sexual abuse, etc. [15]. Abrasions can also provide valuable information on the shape of the instruments that caused it. Like all traumatic injuries, bruises require, however, careful consideration and interpretation by the expert, as there are multiple medicolegal problems that can involve. For example, ecchymosis can be of external (traumatic) or internal (stress) cause. They can appear at the place where the blunt instrument was applied. However, there are exceptions: subconjunctival bruises in situations of fracture of the skull base. Importance of abrasions in forensics: always reflects the site of impact; often indicates the causative agent; often indicates the direction of impact; helps in determining the time of injury; and helps in determining the time of injury.

Consider the following story

A caregiver claims her 3-year old fell down on the driveway with her arms outstretched. Upon exam, you note that there is an abrasion on both forearms with the v-point at the bottom. This story is consistent with the caregiver's story. They may be seen in conjunction with contusions and lacerations because forces sufficient to produce scraping may distort underlying soft tissues enough to damage blood vessels to the point of leakage or can actually tear soft tissues.

Since abrasions are not life-threatening, they are often overlooked or ignored. However, form and appearance should be noted in medicolegal cases because they often help investigators interpret the mechanism and circumstances of the injury.

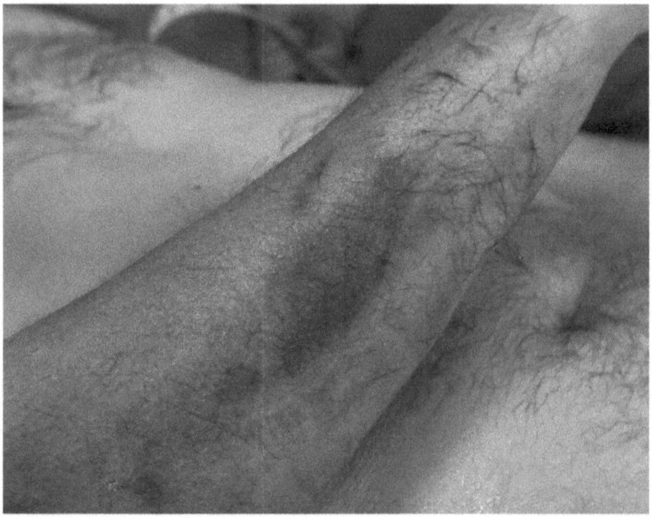

Picture 5—abrasion wound.

Fingernail abrasions

These are important because of their frequency in assaults, especially child abuse, sexual attacks, and strangulations. Often associated with focal bruises. Fingernail abrasions are most often seen on the neck, face, and upper arms and forearm.

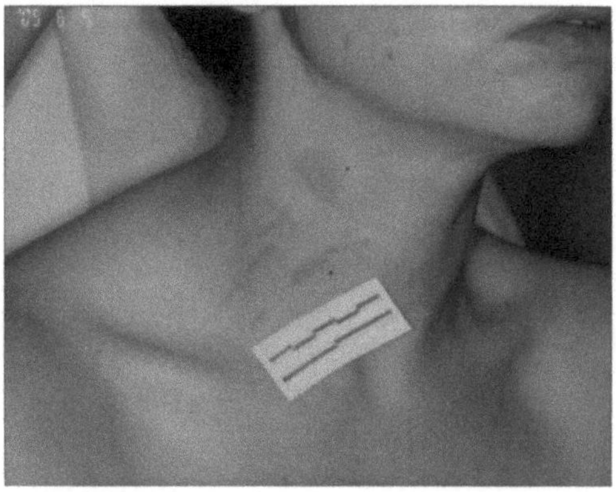

Picture 6—fingernail abrasions.

Bite marks

Bite marks are a form of patterned blunt injury and important to recognize since they are frequently associated with child abuse and sexual assault. They are easy to miss in routine assessments because the imprint is not obvious. Typically, a bite mark is only a contusion but in some cases, there may be abrasions from the teeth scratching the skin. It is easy to confuse a human bite mark with one from an animal. Typically a human bite mark is ovoid-shaped, whereas an animal bite mark is more elliptical. Animal bite marks typically have puncture wounds from the incisor teeth of canines, felines, and other small animals, whereas human bite marks rarely have puncture wounds.

A classic bite mark injury has the following characteristics:

- well-delineated arch
- individual tooth injury
- specific dentition characteristics

It is critical to photograph a suspected bite mark and to swab for DNA recovery.

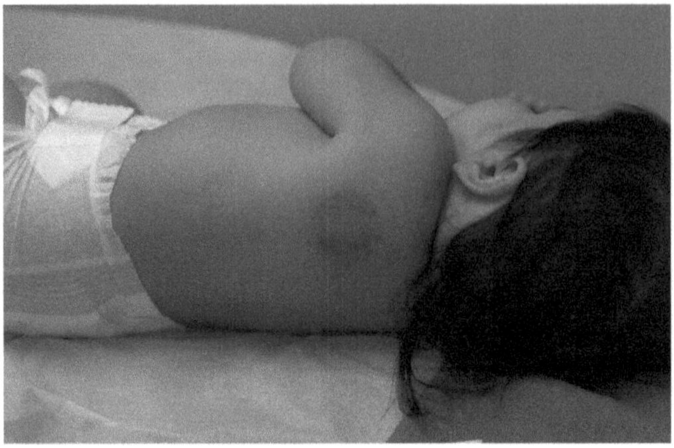

Picture 7—bite marks.

Lacerations

Lacerations are often improperly defined and used, even within the healthcare community. Lacerations are not cuts; they are the result of blunt trauma. They are defects in the soft tissues resulting from tearing, ripping, crushing, overstretching, pulling apart, or shearing. They have irregular margins that may be scraped or bruised. Frequently you can observe "bridging," meaning that the vessels and tissues are not completely torn but are still connected by a bridge of tissue from one side of the laceration to the other. Frequently lacerations contain foreign matter such as glass, dirt, and fibers.

Tears resulting from forceful contact with angular objects can (if there is underlying bone) appear to be a linear injury and may be mistaken for a cut or incised wound. Lacerations may show the direction of force (i.e., v-type wounds—the bottom of the v points in the direction force was applied). Crushed tissues may bleed less and tend to become easily infected.

Medicolegal importance: Shape and size not usually related to causal; rarely self-inflected; trace evidenced in wound (rust or dirt).

Sharp injuries

Sharp injuries are the second major category of traumatic wounds. Each type of sharp injury has its unique features, but there are some similarities among them. Sharp injuries are caused by an object piercing the skin and/or underlying tissue, muscle, bone, and organs of a person. Many tools or weapons can cause sharp injuries, such as knives, guns, scissors, or even pencils. Sharp injuries consist of two subcategories. These are incised wounds (or cuts or incisions) and stab wounds.

The cutting instruments cause the following types of wounds: incised wound, with flap and mutilating, resulting in its action by the “edge” or cut, which can be by simple pressure, or by pressure and sliding, a circumstance, which increases the penetration capacity of the instrument.

The sharp instruments are made up of a thin blade, of triangular section, which acts by the action of the edge and, at the same time, pierces the tissues, damaging several structures along the path. Its mechanism of action leads to the production of injuries that simultaneously bring together characteristics of injuries by sharp and piercing instruments. The punch-blunt instruments, in turn, are constituted by a thin blade, cylindrical or triangular in section, which perforates the tissues and simultaneously produces contusion of the edges. The mechanism of action simultaneously passes here through the characteristics of the piercing and blunt objects [15].

Incised wounds

Incised wounds result from sharp objects coming into contact against the skin and, with pressure, cause injury. Typically, they are longer than they are deep. These are commonly referred to as “cuts.” There is no bridging with incised wounds. Sometimes a cut may not cut through a structure entirely (due to a dull knife, etc.) but leaves a small linear mark thereby confirming a sharp injury. They have clean cut edges without abrasions or bruising. Overlying hair or other small structures within the skin may be cut if the object is sufficiently sharp. There is a scarcity or the absence of foreign material unless something like glass is used as the instrument.

Incised wounds tend to bleed freely unless vessels are completely divided and able to retract. They may be deeper at one end versus the other. They may be irregular if the cut goes through loose skin or affected by clothing. This is another reason why it is important to save the clothing from any patient you suspect is abused or neglected. Clothing can verify or destroy a patient or caregiver’s history.

The incised wound occurs when the instrument penetrates the tissues in a direction more or less perpendicular to the surface of the body. The flap wound occurs when the instrument, having penetrated obliquely, leaves a flap cut in bevel hanging from the body, attached by one end. In the mutilating wound, the instrument crosses the tissues from side to side, highlighting a certain part of the body that is protruding, such as the pinna or the tip of the nose[4].

Incised wounds have some medicolegal problems. The example type: the characteristics of the wound may make it possible to identify, in a "generic" way, the cutting instrument, but they rarely specify, let alone individualize, the same. They can also help to clarify the circumstances and etiology that led to death, given their number, location, depth, being an example for diagnosis of active and passive defense wounds.

Stab wounds

Stab wounds result from visibly sharp and/or pointed objects forced inward by a thrust, fall, or movement. Depth of stab wounds typically exceeds width. Because of this, there is danger to vital internal organs

[4] Blunt injuries: they are injuries produced by the action of blunt instruments, in which, in addition to existing superficial or deep injuries, the skin's elasticity is overcome, becoming a mixture of wound and contusion. Short-blunt injuries—These are mixed injuries, with some characteristics of incised injuries, but produced by the blunt action mechanism (pressure without sliding). When the object has, in addition, a sharp edge, it can cause wounds that are similar to the incised ones, but without sliding action. In this type of injury, the object's mass is associated with a sharp edge and, as such, its edge acts in conjunction with the object's weight, causing very devastating injuries, cutting segments, fracturing or sectioning bones, etc.

Incised or cutting wounds: an incised wound is a break in the continuity of the tissues, resulting from contact with a sharp object. These objects act through a sharp blade that slides over the tissues, separating them. This type of wound exhibits regular edges and well-defined margins, in which the tissue is completely separated, with no abrasions or bruises around the wound or tissue bridges. It is typically a very shallow wound with a high degree of bleeding, as it dissects blood vessels. According to Lacassagne "cutting instruments are those that cut the fabrics in a straight line, causing wounds that are longer than wide, with sharp edges and sharp angles." The wound provides very little information about the vulnerable instrument that caused it; however, it is possible to assess whether the instrument acted perpendicularly or obliquely in relation to the body, the first action producing a simple continuity solution that, due to the elasticity of the sectioned tissues, causes the wound to open, acquiring a shape enlarged oval with superficial ends.

Sharps injuries: these are injuries typically produced by sharp objects, with a sharp blade and edge, such as knives and daggers, better known as "bladed weapons." The type of action these instruments use can be described as a mix between pressure, from the sharp edge, to perforate the fabric, and sliding, from the blade, to cut the fabric. In this type of injury, there is a predominance of depth, at one end, over width and length. The appearance on the surface of the skin is reflected by a regular slit with a rounded tip and the other at an acute angle: in the case of single-cutting instruments, with a knife-edge, two sharp-angled ends; in the case of double-edged instruments, double-edged like the dagger, or in the form of a triangle or star, when the instrument has multiple edges.

and extensive bleeding may be induced. The wound often reflects the characteristics of the wounding instrument. (i.e., single-edged vs double-edged knife). There is relatively little abrasion potential unless the wound is tapering and wedges/stretches the skin on the way in. Occasionally, fragments from the cutting tool will remain in the wound.

Again, save the clothing of any patient with stab wounds. Not only clothing is an important clue to the actual events but it can also contain trace evidence a crime lab technician can find under a microscopic examination. This trace evidence can be incredibly useful to investigators in verifying that a crime actually occurred and can lead to prosecution and incarceration.

With knife stab wounds you can sometimes determine what type of weapon (i.e., single edge, double edge, or serrated edge) caused the wound based on the appearance. The above photo shows stab wounds with a single-edged blade. One end of the wound is rounded, whereas the other end is more slit-like. If this had been a double edge blade, both ends of the wound would be slit-like.

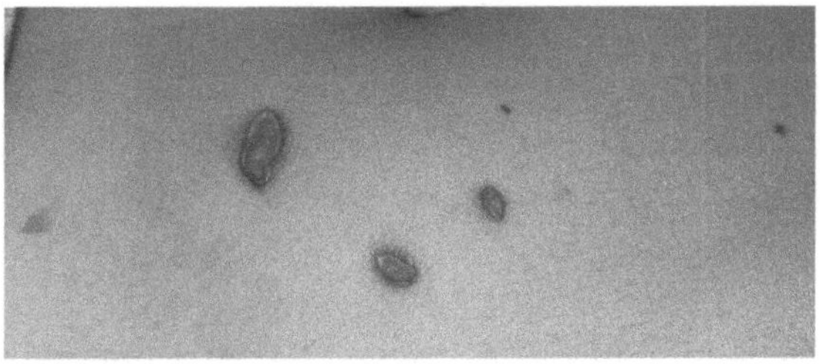

Picture 8—stab wounds.

Mixed: blunt and sharp

Sometimes you will come across wounds that are not solely blunt or sharp. These wounds occur with semisharp or semiblunt objects, like old axes, being ejected into crushed rock or falling onto scrap metal. Once you can determine between blunt and sharp injuries, you can easily identify the mixed wounds.

Perforating instruments—These are simple, long, pointed, and have a small transverse diameter. They penetrate the tissue, removing the respective fibers, depending on the characteristics of the wound, thus totally on the muscle fibers and not on the instrument. The resulting wounds are commonly called "puncture wounds" and can be superficial or deep. Deep (or penetrating) wounds can also be classified as cavitary (when the instrument reaches one of the three cavities—head, chest, and abdomen), transfixing, and impaling.

Piercing or puncturing injuries—This type of injury is typically produced by long, thin, and sharp instruments, which act by pressure, piercing the skin, dissociating, and moving away the anatomical elements of the perforated tissue, often overcoming the elastic limits of that tissue. The lesion is characterized by a small cylindrical point/hole in the affected tissue, being considered that typical wound that transfixes the total thickness of a tissue or organ, such as the skin. In this type of injury, we can verify that there is a marked domain of depth in relation to the surface dimensions (length and width), that is, it is a typically deep injury, leaving only a small wound, usually cylindrical, or even almost imperceptible (in the case of weapons like needles and pins).

Blunt piercing wounds are produced by a mechanism of action that pierces and bruises at the same time. Most of the time, these instruments are more piercing than blunt. These injuries are almost always produced by firearm projectiles; however, they can be represented by similar means, such as the tip of an umbrella. This type of injury is very characteristic of injuries produced by firearm projectiles, and practically all authors, when referring to blunt-wound injuries, proceed automatically to an explanatory explanation of the characteristics of firearms and the type of injuries they cause. To understand these firearm injuries, it is necessary to acquire some basic knowledge about the characteristics and mechanisms of the various existing weapons and their projectiles.

Self-inflicted injuries

Cuts are usually superficial, multiple, and parallel. In right-handed people, most of the injuries are on the left side.

Defense wounds

A wound is sustained when a victim places a hand, arm, or other body parts to prevent or minimize a blow or slashing by a sharp weapon. Usual sites: the outer side of the forearm; back of the hand; fingers;

bruises may be seen at the outer side of the thigh as the victim crosses his legs to protect the genitalia.

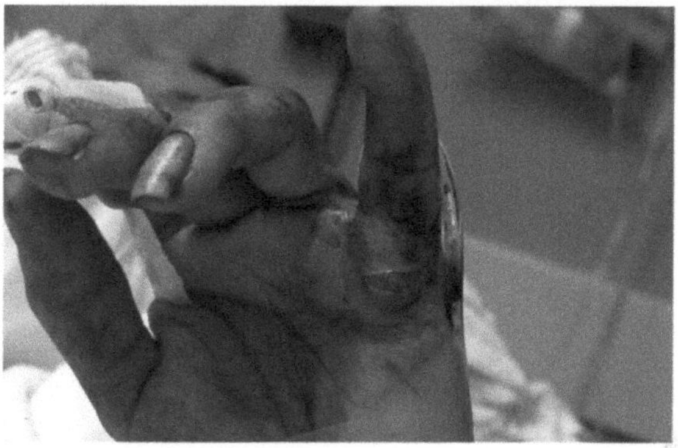

Picture 9—hand defense wounds.

Strangulation/restraint

When an infant or young child is persistently crying and the caregiver attempts to muffle the sounds, they may strangle or throttle, smother, or suffocate the child. The mechanical forces involved in these acts are separate and distinct. They all can result in asphyxia, or a lack of essential oxygen because the structures and processes required for breathing are impaired. After death, in some cases, it may be difficult to distinguish which mechanism induced the fatal asphyxia. However, with infants and children who are still alive, but injured, it is imperative to search for clues left behind including patterned abrasions or ligature marks. Petechiae (small pinpoint or spot-like red areas of bleeding that are clustered beneath the skin and membranes) are also associated with asphyxia. Petechiae result from the bursting of capillaries under the skin.

More terms and definitions

We have already covered an abundance of terminology. There are a few more terms, however, you should be familiar with for proper documentation of forensic evidence.

Avulsions: forceful separation or detachment; tearing away of a body part.

Blister/friction blister: formed by shearing between the more superficial and deeper skin structures, which causes a cleft or split (usually

in the basal cells in/below the granular layer of skin) which then allows fluid to flow; usually occurs on hands and feet.
Chop wounds: deep, gaping wounds often involving major structures, resulting from the use of heavy, sharp objects like cleavers.
Pattern of injury: combination or distribution of external/internal injuries, which suggest a causative mechanism or sequence of events.
Patterned injury: injury which possesses features or configurations indicative of the object or surface that produced it (i.e., hand imprint from a slap, radiator marks).
Penetrating injury: one that enters but does not exit.
Perforating injury: one that enters and exits (a through and through).

External physical agents

The physical agents include heat, cold, electricity, and radiation. Regarding heat, injuries are usually caused by the action of fire (which can cause burns of different degrees) and also by boiling liquids, solid objects, red metals, gases, and vapors. I will address the characteristics of the different agents below.

External chemical agents

External chemical agents include injuries caused by contact with the skin or mucous membranes of chemical substances that cause cell necrosis. At resulting burns have the same degree throughout its extension area, being known as "chemical burns."

External toxic agents

Within the toxic external agents, there are substances that cause changes in the body's biochemical elements fundamental to life. They can act on the cell, producing a global destruction of it, by necrosis processes, or on the enzymatic system, or selective parts of the cell. There are three types of poisoning: acute, subacute, and chronic. Acute intoxications consist of those in which there is a short-term exposure, in a single dose or multiple doses, but in a short time and with rapid absorption of the toxic. Subcutis consists of frequent or repeated exposure for several days or weeks before the symptoms of intoxication appear. Finally, in the chronic intoxication, there is a repeated exposure over a long period of time, which causes the intoxication to manifest only after there is an accumulation of small doses of toxic.

Causes and mechanisms in violent death

Cause of death is any injury or disease that produces a physiological derangement in the body that results in the death of the individual.

Wounds can be grouped into two types: so-called primary injuries, that is, those that result directly from external violence; and those designated as secondary injuries, those that result from reactions or complications of primary injuries. There is a relationship between the mechanisms (direct or indirect) of death and the speed with which it occurs.

A direct cause is defined as the pathological state or traumatic injury that directly caused death, that is, that triggered the agonistic mechanisms. In both situations, death mechanisms are excluded, which are defined as the irreversible changes in vital functions. Likewise, both, illness or traumatic injury, correspond to the ultimate consequence of the underlying cause.

The pathological state that relates the basic cause to the direct cause, when it exists, is defined as an intermediate cause. If not, there is only room for discrimination against the other two. In the case of violent deaths, it corresponds to the external agent that produced the traumatic injuries.

The basic cause is defined, in natural death, as that in which the pathological state is responsible for the triggering of other pathological states classifiable as a direct cause, that is, the disease that triggers the agonic mechanisms.

In this sense, Arsénio Nunes considered that rapid violent death occurs quickly after the action of external violence by mechanisms directly related to primary injuries. He also considered that late violent death occurs after a certain period of time by indirect mechanisms. Note that the difference between cause and mechanism of death, from a medicolegal point of view, is based on the fact that the cause of death is the primary lesion that triggered the pathophysiological changes leading to death, whereas the mechanism of death is understood as the pathophysiological alteration incompatible with life, which may be, in this case, a direct or indirect mechanism. In immediate violent death, injuries alone give way to death, acting through three mechanisms:

1. destruction of a vital organ or functional injury to an organ essential to life. When the destruction is anatomically evident, the diagnosis does not pose major problems.
2. Hemorrhage—hemorrhage, whether internal or external, can be a mechanism of rapid violent death, when a large volume of blood is lost in a short time, leading to hypovolemic shock.
3. Shock—the primary injuries that most often lead to death from shock are extensive injuries, which do not affect vital organs.

In late violent death, the mechanisms of death are indirect and triggered (being aggravated by the action of external violence). The main mechanisms by which an injury, resulting from external violence, can lead to late death are infection, embolisms, asphyxia, and cardiovascular changes.

The mechanism of death is the physiological derangement produced by the cause of death that results in death. The manner of death explains how the cause of death came about. Manners of death can generally be categorized as natural, homicide, suicide, accident, or undetermined.

CHAPTER 5

Violent death in emergency department and prehospital

The cases of violent death, which occur in the prehospital context, are, overall, identical to deaths that occur in the hospital context. We will briefly analyze the situations of violent death that occur most frequently, and which, as such, will be more frequently observed in these contexts.

Death caused by external mechanical agents

Firearms injuries

Gun

The holder presses the firing pin that in turn strikes the primer which ignites the powder and produces large amount of hot gas, produces very high pressure that fires the bullet forcefully through the barrel, leaving the muzzle, and onto the target.

Mechanism of injury

As the missile traverses the body, it causes injury by basic contact of bullet and its fragments (if present) with the tissue. A larger bullet causes bigger damage at the same velocity. Transferring some of the bullet's available kinetic energy to the tissue around it greatly increases damage when velocity is increased. It also causes cavitations in the tissue it passes as it accelerates molecules (makes them move centrifugally away from the axis of the bullet). Bullets do not typically follow a straight line to the target. Rotational forces are in effect that keeps the bullet off a straight axis of flight.

Firearms act as blunt instruments. The projectile, when passing through the skin, produces a cavity. The size and shape of the cavity are caused by their kinetic energy [17]. The entrance wound may

EMS in Crime Scene. DOI: https://doi.org/10.1016/B978-0-12-824420-3.00003-4

involve an abrasive injury[1] and a bruise ring, the bruise ring being caused by the skin's resistance to bullet entry. Around the entry wound, powder residue may remain, creating a tattoo. Only entry wounds have these characteristics.

Mode of injury depends on the velocity of the missile: slow velocity is lower than 340 m/s and high velocity is around 1500 m/s. High-velocity missile creates a shockwave around its track (severe disruption), increases the tissue pressure, and causes more damage. So, a 10 mm wide bullet may cause a 15 mm wide track of damage.

The health professional who first comes into contact with the firearm injury must note all the characteristics of the injury (location, diameter of the hole). Tattoos help determine the distance from which the shot was fired and may have unburned gunpowder particles. Ideally, you should photograph and draw the location on the body diagram.

Weapons can be classified according to their constitution into typical and atypical, and according to the length of the barrel and range, into short and long. As typical weapons, we have commercial weapons manufactured in series, with a rigor that allows establishing specificities and comparisons for each type (range, projectile speed, impact power, etc.). As atypical weapons, there are rudimentary and improvised weapons, made manually, without technical rigor, including the typical ones whose essential characteristics have been altered, for which, due to their irregular behavior, it is not possible to determine specifics and comparisons. In this type of assault with firearms, the determination of distance is one of the essential elements for the purposes of accountability.

[1] Contusion ring—During the projectile's penetration process, the skin tends to conform to the projectile and, as a consequence, creates an eroded area. This is partly due to the projectile's friction with the skin associated with the projectile's rotation movement, and partly due to the difference in elasticity between the dermis and the epidermis, which results in the plucking of the epidermis, forming a bruised or bruised oral (contusion border). The analysis of this erosion allows a series of information regarding the trajectory.

Barrel: the metal tube through which the bullet is fired.

Bore: the inside of the barrel, either Smoothbore.

Muzzle: the end of the barrel out of which the bullet comes out.

Primer: volatile substance that ignites when struck to detonate the powder in a cartridge.

Smoothbore weapon (Shotgun): A gun with a smoothbore that shoots cartridges that contain "shot" or small metal pellets (of lead or steel) as the projectiles.

As short weapons, we have, for example, pistols and revolvers; as long weapons, we find shotguns, rifles, and machine guns. It is important to know that, during the firing of ammunition, there are materials that are released. In this case, we can find combustion and explosion gases, black smoke, powder grains (burned or not), the projectile (single or multiple), the casing (capsule or cartridge), and bushings (in the case of shotguns).

Thus we can divide the components and materials triggered into:

1. Projectile
   a. single, in fluted barrel weapons (pistols, revolver, carabine, etc.);
   b. multiple, in smoothbore weapons (shotguns), which can also make single-projectile shots.
2. Enclosure
   a. metallic capsule (fluted-barrel weapons);
   b. plastic or cardboard cartridge (shotguns).
3. Bushings used only in cartridges, to separate the powder from the lead, or to close the ammunition.
4. Gases are released through the muzzle of the gun, as a result of explosive combustion of gunpowder.
5. Flame: small cone, at the muzzle of the gun, as a result of combustion of gunpowder.
6. Carbon black: black or grayish color, depending on the type of powder, resulting from said combustion.
7. In combusted gunpowder: grains or blades of gunpowder, which did not burn, are projected through the muzzle, in the form of a short-reaching cone.

Ammunition: A shotgun shell (cartridge) may contain one large projectile (called a slug), a few pellets of large shot, or many tiny pellets. Cartridge made of a cylinder fitted into a metal base contains charge of propellant, wads, and shots. Range is the most important factor and can be estimated in over half of the cases. Close range wounds are severe, but at even relatively short distances, wounding may be minimal.

Solid organs such as the brain and the liver are affected more than the spongy lung. In most of the shooting cases seen by forensic pathologists, death will have occurred rapidly, however when it is delayed secondary damage from infarction, local necrosis of muscles and organs, and infections must always be kept in mind.

Regarding the characteristics of the injuries sustained by a firearm, the form of entry will depend on multiple circumstances, such as the nature of the weapon projectile, the distance and incidence of the shot, and the existence or not of intermediate targets [15].

Entrance orifice: In general, the entrance orifice is small, with an abrasion collar due to the heat of the bullet's friction when it penetrates the skin. The exit wound is usually larger, and the skin can be projected from the inside out, in the shape of a star. If the projectile has hit the bone in its path, it may disintegrate and help form a much larger hole.

At the level of the holes caused by the projectiles, an assessment of the victim's clothing and body should be carried out. In clothing, attention should be paid to the detection of evidences of singed hole, as well as the presence of carbon black, and gunpowder. In the victim's body, in addition to these, the existence or not of:

- cleaning edge—dark debris (dirt inside the pipe, oil, etc.) that the projectile leaves, trapped in the skin that surrounds the space immediately after the entrance hole;
- contusion border—a lesion located around the cleaning border, resulting from the punch-blunt impact against the body;
- in short-range shots (contact shots and at close range), the burn (resulting from the flame cone), smoke and incombustible gunpowder particles, as well as black of carbon black, can be detected inside the projectile's penetration channel or at its edges.

Most entrance wounds, no matter the range, are surrounded by a reddish, reddish-brown zone of abraded skin (the abrasion ring).

The entrance wounds have the following characteristics:

- Central defect—The diameter approximates that of the penetrating projectile. The head of the projectile causes tissue destruction on impact, whilst the periphery suffers irreversible compression.
- Ring of dirt—Due to black powder residue, gun oil, or dirt rubbed off the projectile during penetration, comes from the head of the bullet—not the body (which does not contact the wound edges).
- Abrasion ring—Symmetrical, concentric ring around the central defect during a head-on impact of the projectile. This is a rim of flattened, abraded epidermis, surrounding the entrance hole. Fresh

entrance wounds have an abrasion ring with a moist, fleshy appearance. As the abrasion ring dries out, however, it assumes the more familiar appearance. The abrasion ring is also not due to the bullet burning the skin.
- Inverted edges—The skin moves away from the projectile, upon impact. It bulges outward and the temporary entrance hole contracts after the projectile passes through.

Abrasion ring: The abrasion ring can vary in width, depending on the caliber of the weapon, the angle at which the bullet entered, and the anatomic site of the entrance. Abrasion rings may have very unusual configurations.

Equimotic areola: The ecchymosis is an infiltration of blood resulting from the rupture of capillaries, caused by the passage of the projectile. The equimotic areola is formed around the entrance orifice and presents a variable color over time, that is, over time, it becomes accentuated to a darkened purple tone. It is important to remember that the equimotic halo is a vital reaction; therefore it allows defining postmortem injuries that do not show this sign.

Tattoos:[2] Drawings or figures, in the form of circles or ovals, of greater or lesser dimension (depending on the distance at which the shot was made), which are engraved on the skin, around the entrance orifice.

[2] Tattoo zone—It is produced by the inlay of the grains of incombustible gunpowder, which reach the target around the entrance orifice, as well as small fragments that come off the projectile. It is due to the greater mass and greater kinetic energy, that the other firing residues, such as gases and products of combustion, reach greater distances and penetrate the surface of the target, as microprojectiles, embedded in it more or less deeply, not being removable by washing. The greater the distance between the muzzle of the gun and the holder, the less deep the encrustation will be. Some experts propose a subdivision of the tattoo zone into: Indelible Tattoo, when the encrustation occurs in deeper layers, not leaving with water or superficial washing, that is, the tattoo area itself, and Eerie Tattoo, when there is only a deposition (adherence) of the grain on the surface of the skin without encrusting, it can be removed by a simple wash.

Rim edge—The projectile carries dirt attached to it, from its passage through the gun barrel. When reaching a flexible target like human skin, it usually adheres to this surface and, in part, surrounds the projectile, resulting in the "cleaning" of the projectile at the edges of the support surface. Residues or dirt left on the skin characterize the wiping edge. The drying edge is concentric in the perpendicular and arciform (arc-shaped) or elliptical in oblique shots. The shade depends on the substances that are adhered to the projectile and is usually dark. It should be noted that on the most resistant surfaces deposition of the metal alloy that makes up the projectile occurs, especially on those whose main element is lead.

An entrance orifice does not necessarily correspond to an exit orifice [18]. The absence of an exit orifice may imply the recovery of the projectile during the autopsy (depending on its location) [18]. It should be noted that the streaks molded on the projectile, as well as the marks left on the capsule, as a result of its percussion, may allow the performance of laboratory tests by comparison (test shots), which lead to the identification of the weapon responsible for the crime.

Exit orifice: The exit wound is usually larger, breaking the skin from the inside out, in the shape of a star. If the projectile has hit a bone, it may disintegrate, forming a large orifice. Sometimes, if the skin is tied by a belt or a tight garment, or even if the victim is leaning against a wall, the outgoing wound can be as small as the incoming wound. In this type of orifice, there are no bruising and cleaning edges, but, as a rule, it has larger dimensions than the entrance, with irregular, star-shaped contours. At the same time, bleeding is greater and there may be adipose/bone tissue in the orifice. Exit wounds, whether they are the result of contact, intermediate, or distant firing, all have the same general characteristics.

Shooting distance: In general, we can say that, in relation to firearms, there are four types of shooting distance: contact shooting, point-blank shooting, short-distance shooting, and long-distance shooting.

Classification of wound distances according to Di Maio (27):

Classification of entrance wounds

We can classify *rifle entrance* wounds according to the range of fire into

1. contact wound
2. close range wound (up to 20 cm)
3. intermediate wound(20 cm–1 m)
4. distant range wound (over 1 m)

Contact wound

When a weapon is fired in contact with the skin. The appearances can vary according to whether the muzzle was firmly pressed against the surface to form a tight seal, appears more like shotgun loose contact so that the backward jerk of recoil can permit a small gap to appear. Most rifled weapon ammunition is “clean,” compared with many shotgun cartridges, so that soot may be absent altogether.

A contact wound is one in which the muzzle of the weapon is held against the body at the time of discharge. Contact wounds can be hard, loose, angled, or incomplete. In contact wounds gas, soot, metallic particles avulsed from the bullet by the rifling, vaporized metal from the bullet and cartridge case, primer residue, and powder particles are all driven into the wound track along with the bullet (27).

Contact wound over a bony support: usually the skull. Contact wounds in regions of the body where only a thin layer of skin and subcutaneous tissue overlies bone usually have a stellate or cruciform appearance that is totally unlike the round or oval perforating wounds seen in other areas. The muzzle gases entering the subcutaneous tissues cannot expand by displacing adjacent soft structures and are reflected from the bone to raise a dome of gas that often splits the entry hole. This results in a linear, cruciate, or stellate tear that may well destroy the original puncture. In some contact wounds over bone, instead of the classical stellate or cruciform wound, one finds a very large circular wound with ragged, blackened, and seared margins (27).

Close-range wounds

When there is a short distance between the muzzle and body surface. The appearance of the wound will vary accordingly to the type of ammunition used. Near-contact wounds lie in a gray zone between contact and intermediate-range wounds. In near-contact wounds, the muzzle of the weapon is not in contact with the skin, being held a short distance away. The distance, however, is so small that the powder grains emerging from the muzzle do not have a chance to disperse and mark the skin, producing the powder tattooing that is the sine qua non of intermediate-range wounds (27).

The wound appearance

- will almost invariably be circular;
- no tearing;
- the wound edges may be inverted;
- entrance wound: regular edge orifice, charred edge, smoke black edge.

Medium distance wounds

Once the discharge of a rifled weapon is greater than a meter, there is nothing to indicate increasing range. An intermediate-range gunshot wound is one in which the muzzle of the weapon is away from the body at the time of discharge yet is sufficiently close so that powder grains emerging from the muzzle strike the skin producing powder tattooing; this is the sine qua non of intermediate-range gunshot wounds. The typical appearance of the entry wound has been likened to that caused by "driving a dirty pencil through the skin." Abrasion collar appearance.

Distant wounds

In distant gunshot wounds, the muzzle of the weapon is sufficiently far from the body so that there is neither deposition of soot nor powder tattooing.

Clothing will absorb soot and powder, in some cases making close-range wounds appear to be distant by examination of the body alone. This points out the need for examination of the clothing in conjunction with the autopsy. The presence of isolated powder particles on either the clothing or the body does not necessarily signify that one is dealing with an intermediate-range wound, as individual powder particles may travel considerable distances before deposition on the body (27).

Range determinations cannot be made for distant gunshot wounds.

Exit wounds from rifled weapons

The muzzle velocity is important in determining whether a single bullet will completely traverse the body. In general, they are characterized by:

- usually larger than entrance wounds;
- irregularly shaped;
- everted skin edges;
- no powder tattooing, soot soiling or stippling, etc.;
- may have abraded edges;

Unlike fluted-barreled weapons, which fire a single projectile at a time, a shotgun fires ammunition (cartridge), which may contain a variable number of projectiles, spherical (berries), which in turn can range from 1 to 850. When firing, the berries remain clustered up to about 3 m, and then they are dispersed in a cone shape.

The end of the barrel (there are shotguns with two pipes, juxtaposed or overlapping) presents a variable strangulation, which allows a variable agglutination of the projectiles. The greater the strangulation, the greater the distance over which the berries remain clustered. In the shotguns with two pipes, each one has a different choke, causing different dispersions.

In the shotgun weapon, the calculation of the distance at which the weapon was fired is carried out by studying the dispersion of the berries, a dispersion that depends on the quality of the powder, the number of berries (more berries, greater dispersion), and the type of bushings (agglutinators and dispersers). In cases involving shotgun rifles, the plastic bush must be recovered, without causing significant changes to its shape (it is a determining element in determining the firing distance) and the largest possible number of lead berries, (for test examinations for the determination of the range of possible shooting distances).

Estimation of shooting distance
In forensic medicine, three ranges of fire are distinguished according to morphological criteria:

- contact range
- short/close and medium/intermediate range
- long/distant range.

Gunshot wounds types
- Penetrating wounds: which only have an entrance wound;
- Perforating wounds: which have both entrance and exit wounds.

Characteristics of entrance wounds
- Punched-out hole in the skin (rounded vs oval). However, the diameter is usually smaller than that of the bullet. (After the bullet enters through the skin, the skin retracts due to its elasticity. This will make the wound appear smaller than the bullet that has passed through.)
- Marginal zone without epidermis and small amounts of blood escape through (abrasion ring).
- Grayish-black ring of dirt.

Characteristics of exit wounds
- Usually, the size is larger than that of the entry wound;
- irregular;
- with extruding tissue but no abrasion margin;
- more blood escapes from the exit wound.

Classification of entrance wounds in relation to the range from muzzle to target

Three ranges of fire are distinguished according to morphological criteria:

1. contact range
2. short/close and medium/intermediate range
3. long/distant range.

Contact range (shots)

The muzzle was held against the body surface at the time of discharge. The entrance wound will be single, circular and about the size of the muzzle. The combustion gases have a high content of CO (up to 50%), the surrounding tissue often assumes a bright cherry-red color. If the entrance wound is above a bony support, the subcutaneous expansion of the penetrating gases may cause radial skin tears due to overstretching, resulting in a stellate wound of entrance.

Distance: gun muzzle against the target (0 cm). "In closed cavity" – the destructive effects of the projectile are added to those produced by the (internal) expansion of the gas chamber.

Characteristics

- Entrance wound: starry orifice, with irregular and lacerated contours (usually smaller than the exit);
- carbon black on the edges of the hole (deposited fumes, easily washable);
- burning or scorching the edges;
- stamping (possible) of the gun's mouth (especially in automatic weapons);
- leaning shot can produce an impression on the skin which is known as the Werkgartner sign[3].

[3] Werkgartner sign – It is the burn injury, produced by the barrel of the gun still hot, to the point of printing on the victim's skin the circular mark of the barrel and, in some cases, marks of other characteristics that the weapon has, such as example, sight mass, actual spring guide, front of frame in the pistols, since the smoke, depending on the type and characteristics of the propellant used, may not be well noticed by the expert. It is noteworthy that the means of production of this signal is different from that which produces the flame zone, that is, it is produced by the flame arising from the high temperature of the gases when it expands, whereas the Werkgartner signal is the result of skin contact with the heated (gun) barrel.

Benassi sign—It is the smoke deposit (smoke) in the bony plane, around and in the entrance orifice, which occurs when shots are fired with the end of the gun barrel (mouth) against the skin that covers a bone plate. It is very useful, when the soft parts are rotting or do not exist, to

Close range shots
No muzzle mark. Burning of the skin with blistering. Tissue within and around the wound is cherry pink due to CO. The wound is surrounded by large defect of "stippling" or "tattooing." The distribution pattern of powder tattooing/stippling varies according to the angle of fire.

Distance: gun muzzle up to 1 cm from the target (usually no higher than the flame cone).

Intermediate range shots
Distance: mouth of the weapon from 1 to 75 cm from the target (in general, no higher than the flame cone).

Entrance wound: circular or oval hole, with regular edges, cleaning border, contusion border (appears after 6–8 hours), tattoo characteristic of these wounds, formed by carbon black (washable part of the shots up to 45 cm), and unburned gunpowder grains (indelible part). Hair and clothing can interfere the appearance of the entrance wound in perpendicular and oblique shots.

Long-distance range shots
Distance: gun mouth more than 75 cm from the target.

Entrance wound: circular or oval hole, with regular edges. It has only a contusion border, the aspect of the wound in perpendicular and oblique shots.

No soot and no powder grains (i.e., no tattooing) could reach the body surface.

identify incoming lesions with the barrel leaning against the target. Hoffmann mine chamber—In situations where the firing occurs against the target covering the bone plate, the gases released in the firing pass through the tissue and, upon reaching the bony bulkhead, detach the tissue from the side and reflect violently, resulting in starring and eversion of the edges of the skin. This process is called "Hofmann Mine Chamber." The velocity of the gases that propel the projectile is 1.5 to 2 times greater than the velocity of the projectile. When a firing occurs against a surface that covers a bone plate, these gases penetrate the lesion and are retained by the projectile, while it pierces the bone plate, thus, they end up expanding laterally between the tissue and that plate, taking off the skin and forming an inflated area, full of gases, which, when refluxing, end up lacerating the tissue in a starry shape, with jagged edges, irregular and often turned outward. The lesion is usually blackened by the deposit of soot from the burning of the propellant.

Shotguns rarely produce an exit wound, but if the shot was in the head, the skull may explode with the gas pressure from a contact wound, ejecting part or even all of the brain from the cranial cavity.

The powder tattooing helps to determine whether or not the victim was alive before the shooting. An examination of the wound can also indicate whether or not the victim was alive when he was shot. If a reddish-brown to orange-red powder tattooing exists, that indicates that the individual was in fact alive when the wound was inflicted. However, if the powder has produced gray or yellow marks instead, the individual was dead before the shooting.

What affects patterns of tissue injury

- Deformation of the bullet;
- fragmentation of the bullet;
- amount of kinetic energy imparted to tissues;
- secondary targets such as bone;
- tissue characteristics affect patterns of tissue injury (the higher the specific gravity of tissue, the greater the damage. While elasticity reduces the damage);
- lung tissue of low density and high elasticity is damaged less than muscle with higher density but some elasticity;
- liver, spleen, brain, and adipose tissue have little tensile strength and elasticity and are easily injured;
- fluid-filled organs (bladder, heart, great vessels, bowel) can burst because of pressure waves generated;
- a bullet striking bone may cause fragmentation of bone and/or bullet, with numerous secondary missiles formed, each producing additional wounding. Fragmentation increases the permanent cavity size.

Shot direction

Regarding the direction of the shot, the analysis is deduced from the following elements:

- Regarding the shape of the contusion edge, it is semilunar on the side from which the projectile came.
- There is a distribution of tattoos that, in the case of entry holes, are oval.
- It depends on the direction of travel.

Injuries produced by tangential action

The injuries caused by tangential shots have specific characteristics and, depending on the degree of engagement of this projectile to the tissue, have different morphologies. In cases where greater contact of the projectile with the skin occurs, it is expected to verify a laceration (groove) in the ditch-shaped fabric, with loss of material through the passage of the projectile caused by abrasive wear.

The edges of these lacerations are totally irregular, showing small superficial grooves, diagonally arranged from the main groove, from which it is possible to determine the trajectory of the projectile. The width of the wound is approximately equivalent to the diameter of the projectile.

There are three factors that are relevant in the formation of the wound [15]: the permanent cavity[4], the formation of secondary projectiles, and the temporary cavity[5] and the phenomenon of cavitation.

Temporary cavitation effects: When the projectile passes at high speed through the tissues, hydraulic shock waves are established in the adjacent aqueous tissues. These shock waves can be transmitted over considerable distances in the body and can result in injury to remote regions in relation to the projectile path. The effect can be more dramatic on organs filled with fluid and air, such as the gallbladder, stomach, liver, spleen, and colon, which can rupture as a result of animated projectile injuries at considerable speeds, even if these projectiles produce (or cause) its permanent cavity away from these organs.

[4] Permanent cavity: As the projectile passes through the tissues, it will present a path of tissue damage, whose diameter will be proportional to the contact area of the projectile that crosses it. This local path, with irreversible loss of tissues, is called a permanent cavity. This phenomenon is always present and is augmented by projectiles of larger caliber, as well as projectiles that expand and "open like a mushroom" when the impact occurs. Expansive projectiles, when animated with a minimum velocity that allows their expansion, have a larger contact area, so a larger permanent cavity is to be expected.

[5] The temporary cavity and the phenomenon of cavitation: In addition to the permanent cavity, another factor to be considered is the temporary cavity. When the interaction of the projectile with the tissue occurs, a greater or lesser distance from the tissues around the projectile path may occur. This momentary compression of the tissues generates a temporary cavity and allows the propagation of shock waves, which can produce tissue damage, extending for several centimeters (in a concentric way) laterally to the projectile and its path. The temporary cavity lasts only a few milliseconds (between 5 and 20 ms), but it can cause damage to structures that are not in its path.

Wound ballistics of the shotgun

At close range, the shotgun is the most formidable and destructive of all small arms. For birdshot and buckshot loads, the severity and lethality of a shotgun wound depend on the number of pellets that enter the body, the organs struck by the pellets, and the amount of tissue destruction (27). Temporary cavities play no significant role in the injury. In shotguns, the range from muzzle to target is extremely important in determining the number of pellets that strike a body and enter it.

Contact shotgun wounds of the head are among the most mutilating firearms wounds there are. Extensive destruction of bone and soft tissue structures with bursting ruptures of the head are the rule rather than the exception. The severity of the injuries in contact wounds of the head is due to two factors: the charge of shot entering the skull and the gas from combustion of the propellant (27). Most contact shotgun wounds of the head are suicidal in origin.

Contact wounds of the trunk appear relatively innocuous when compared with the massive destruction produced by such wounds in the head. The wound of entrance will be circular in shape and will have a diameter approximately equal to that of the bore of the weapon.

As the muzzle of the shotgun is moved farther from the body, tattooing disappears and the diameter of the circular wound of entrance increases in size until a point is reached where individual pellets begin to separate from the main mass.

In all deaths from shotgun wounds, the size of the shot pattern on the body should be measured so that the range can be determined accurately. There have been many formulas published to determine the range at which a shotgun has been discharged, but none of these formulas is reliable. The wound measurements given in the previous paragraphs should be used only as a rough guide in estimating range.

Stab wounds and penetrating injuries

These are of major importance in forensic pathology, as they are extremely common in homicide. A damaging instrument is defined as a bladed weapon which, when handled, acts on the body through a cutting edge and/or tip. The injuries caused by bladed weapons are normally of the sharp type. In this type of instrument, the perforating lesions are characterized by the existence of an entrance orifice (located in the skin, the wound is reddish or rosacea), and a path (channel that crosses different anatomical structures), with or without an orifice.

A stab wound is an incised wound that is deeper than it is wide. Knives are the weapons most frequently involved and their physical characteristics are important in shaping the wound. Other knife-like weapons include scissors, chisels, swords, open razors, and sharp tools of many kinds, including deliberately modified tools such as sharpened screwdrivers. Larger cutting instruments such as axes, choppers, parangs, machetes, and pangas, and agricultural implements such as shears, bill-hooks, hay-knives, and many others have been used as stabbing weapons when used by the point rather than the long edge.

The multiplicity of blows appears both in victims of homicidal attacks and in those resulting from suicidal acts. The specific shape of the wound makes it possible to determine the type of weapon used (e.g., double-edged blade). An injury called a dovetail[6] is common in homicidal situations. During the assault, the blade is driven in one direction and removed in another, because the attacker and/or the victim have changed positions. Seeming to be confluent injuries, it is just the same aggression.

The location of wounds in situations of homicide provides data about the author (left, right, etc.). The existence of injuries caused by more than one instrument points to a homicide situation. In a certain type of suicide, namely through cuts of wrists, multiple injuries are almost always observed.

[6] Dovetail—The three-edged instruments originate wounds with a triangular or starry shape. Sometimes, there is deformation of the entrance orifice, due to the movement of the hand that manipulates the instrument or the victim's own movement, either widening the injury when there is an inclination at the exit, or changing the shape, when there is rotation after being introduced into the body. Thus, due to the movement in these wounds, the length of the wound can be equal to, greater than or less than the width of the instrument blade. This movement of the instrument or the victim produces L-or Y-shaped injuries, also called "dovetail injuries." The appearance of these injuries is due to the fact that the aggressor is driving the blade in one direction and, when removing it (possibly to strike another blow), doing so in another direction or because, in the meantime, the victim has moved.

A forensic examiner called upon to examine a knife that may have been used in an assault should note and measure:

- the length, width, and thickness of the blade;
- whether it is single or double-edged;
- the degree of taper from tip to hilt;
- the nature of the back edge in a single-edged knife (e.g., serrated or squared-off);
- the face of the hilt guard adjacent to the blade;
- any grooving, serration, or forking of the blade;
- most importantly, the sharpness of the edge and especially of the extreme tip of the blade.

The characteristics of a stab wound

The surface and internal appearances of a stab wound allow the pathologist to offer an opinion upon

- the dimensions of the weapon
- the type of weapon
- the taper of the blade
- movement of the knife in the wound
- the depth of the thrust
- the direction of the thrust
- the amount of force used

The dimensions of the knife may be a vital part of the investigation of a homicide when the weapon has been removed from the scene by the assailant. The pathologist can sometimes assist the investigators by telling them, within limits, what size and type of knife to seek. When suspect weapons are recovered, his inspection of them may indicate whether or not they are consistent with having caused the wounds in question.

The length of the wound should be measured to the nearest millimeter as it lies undisturbed on the skin. In most instances the wound will have gaped across the center, to form a long ellipse. The extent of gaping will depend on the anatomical situation, for example, over joints or in the axilla or groin, and whether the axis of the stab is in line with or across the tension of Langer's lines or underlying muscle bundle.

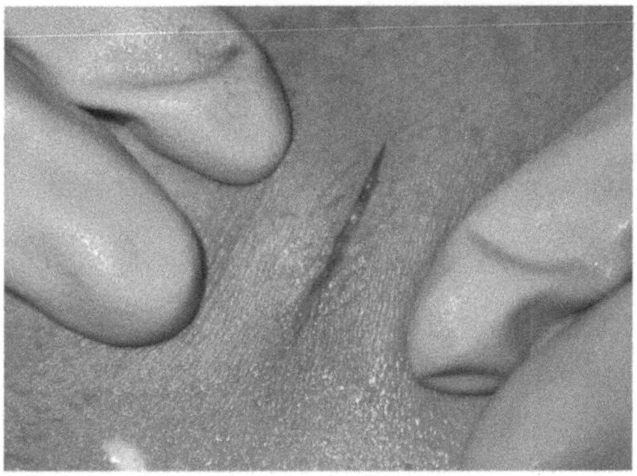

Picture 1 — Approximate the wound edges to measure accurately.

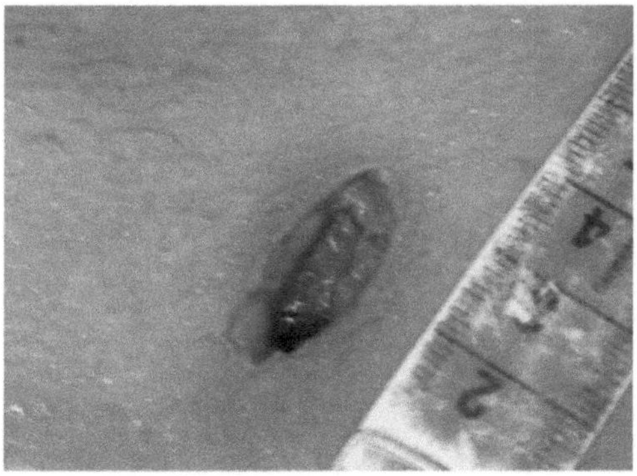

Picture 2 — Wrong measurement of the wound. Extended edges.

Differential diagnosis in stab wounds

The etiology of a stab wound can be accidental, suicidal, or homicidal. However, there is no general guideline that makes it possible, with certainty, to establish the medicolegal differential diagnosis in the face of a wound caused by a melee weapon [15].

The medicolegal differential diagnosis in a stab wound is based on a combination of facts and circumstances that involved it, including particulars imprinted by the weapon on the skin, the type of weapon, the number and order of the wounds, location of the body, the position between the aggressor and the victim, the distance and direction of the injury, the influence of psychotropic substances, personal history and collected evidence [15].

In homicide situations, injuries occur in one or several regions of the body, and in vital or nonvital areas. In suicidal situations, lesions appear almost exclusively in the cardiac region, on the anterior face of the neck and wrists, and as a rule, only one of these regions is affected.

In suicide situations, the injuries have a certain parallelism, due to the fact that the test strokes are delivered under the same angle of incidence (hesitation wound). In homicide situations, the movement of the actors means that such parallelism does not occur, even in injuries located in the same region. There are other deep wounds, which, as a rule, blow in an area higher than that chosen by the suicide bombers.

Differential diagnosis of medicolegal etiology.

Stabbing cases	
Homicide	**Suicide**
• One or more injuries • Variable wound location • Blood on the walls/floor • Broken nails • Dovetail wounds • Hair on the suspect's hands	• As a rule, several injuries, observing trial strokes • Predominance of blows on the left side (in right-handed) • Parallel +/− direction • Scars from previous attempts
Use of one/several instruments	One unique instrument
One or more types of injuries	Typical injuries of the instrument used
Asymmetry in the positioning of wounds	Symmetrical lesions
One or more regions of the body affected, in vital and/or nonvital areas	As a rule, a certain region is reached (often, pulses, heart region, and neck)
Clothes without clearance, but in disarray, lack of buttons, the tears coinciding with injuries	Clothes usually removed. See the position of hands and objects they hold.
Active or passive defense wounds, signs of struggle	There are frequent cases in which, due to marital problems, the man kills the woman and then commits suicide. The murderer sometimes leaves a note to the family, where he declares his "sentence."
Blades nearby or no weapon on the scene	
Absence of weapon on the scene Behavior of domestic animals	

Taper of the blade—The taper of the blade is naturally related to wound size. If a tapered blade is inserted to 4 cm, then the length of the wound (ignoring skin retraction for the moment) will be that of the width of the blade at that level. If the taper continues to the 8 cm level, then the wound will be correspondingly longer. Only when the blade edges become parallel will the wound size remain constant for further penetration of the knife.

Hesitation marks—In self-inflicted incised lesions, hesitation marks are often found. They are mostly due to attempted suicide, attention, gaining courage, or due to indecision. They are also called tentative injuries. These hesitation wounds are superficial adjacent to the incision, continuous and contiguous to it, or overlaid by the fatal incised wound. They are so superficial that they often do not get through the skin. The interpretation of these wounds supports the conclusions that help to clarify between suicide or homicide, as they are self-inflicted. In a suspected suicide, it is always worth observing scars, previous injuries from cuts on the wrists, arms, or neck, compatible with previous attempts. Incised suicidal wounds are usually inflicted on the parts of the body most accessible to the victim. The victim can expose the part of the body where he will cause the incision. For example, you can open your shirt collar before cutting your throat or unbutton your shirt before cutting your chest or abdomen.

In hesitation wounds, the role of the health professional is to assess the characteristics of the injury, as well as all the verifiable variables, so that the documentation he records can later be used in legal matters. The health professional is not asked to make a differential diagnosis about the type of injury he finds, but a detailed description without any ambiguity.

Defense wounds—In assaults of any kind, the natural reaction of the victims is to protect themselves. The limbs used for protection can themselves be injured and these defense wounds may be of considerable medicolegal significance, as they indicate that the victim was conscious, at least partly mobile, and not taken completely by surprise. Defense wounds can be sustained from attacks by fists, feet, and blunt or sharp instruments. The classic position for them is on the forearms and hands, which are instinctively raised to protect the eyes, face, and head. Other defense injuries may be inflicted on the thighs when attempts are made to shield the genitals.

Active defense wounds—In all types of aggression, victims' natural reaction is to protect themselves. The form of defense is to use the members for their protection. The resulting injuries are called defense wounds. These wounds can have considerable medicolegal relevance, as they indicate that the victim was conscious, at least partially mobile and that she was not taken completely by surprise. Defensive wounds are injuries to the extremities incurred when an individual tries to avoid an assault. The classic location of these injuries is on the forearms and hands, which are instinctively raised to protect the eyes, face, and head. They are most commonly found on the front and back of the forearms, on the palms and back of the hands, and the front and back of the fingers. Defense wounds caused by knives cause deep cuts, as the blade tenses through the skin in firm tissues in a tense manner. The cuts are often deep, well-demarcated, with loose skin flaps and heavy bleeding.

Death caused by asphyxia

Asphyxia is a term that literally derives from a Greek word meaning "pulseless" which is commonly understood to mean "lack of oxygen." Asphyxia causes generalized hypoxia, which primarily affects the tissues and organs most sensitive to hypoxia first, such as the brain hence resulting in cerebral hypoxia and death.

We can define asphyxiation situations in which at the cellular level there is partial oxygen deficiency (hypoxia), or the absence of oxygen (anoxia). Mechanical asphyxiation is divided into anoxic anoxia, where we find suffocation, anemic anoxia, where we include hemorrhage and carbon monoxide (CO), circulatory or stagnant anoxia, which occur due to constriction of the neck, and finally the histotoxic anoxias (cyanides). Mechanical asphyxiation presents as general signs of petecheal hemorrhages and congestion, local signs depend on the type of asphyxia.

We can classify asphyxiation into several types. Classically, however, we have the following classification:

- anoxic anoxias (suffocation)
- anemic anoxias (hemorrhage/CO)
- circulatory or stagnant anoxias (constriction of the neck)
- histotoxic anoxias (cyanides)

The general changes caused by asphyxia

- Cyanosis: This is the direct result of oxygen depletion, oxyhemoglobin becoming replaced by reduced hemoglobin. The dark color of the blood as seen through the skin imparts a bluish tinge to the face and other parts of the body. Some degree of peripheral cyanosis is common as to be almost routine in dead bodies—it does not imply asphyxia.

- Edema: In asphyxia, the venous return from the head and neck may be obstructed either directly, from pressure on the neck, or indirectly as a result of an increase in pressure within the chest which stops the blood from entering the heart easily. This causes venous engorgement (congestion) of the face, neck, and also of lungs. The increased hydrostatic pressure within the veins also causes fluid to leak out of the smaller veins into the soft tissues. Soft tissue swelling may also affect the eye sockets, causing the eyes to bulge forwards.
- Petechiae: These are found wherever the vessels are poorly supported. They appear as pinpoints of bleeding within the skin and elsewhere.

Mechanical asphyxia

Mechanical asphyxiation encompasses all situations in which there is an impediment to gas exchange at the alveolar level, in the face of a mechanical obstacle that prevents the access of oxygen to the pulmonary alveoli. Depending on the type of positioning of this obstacle, mechanical asphyxiation can be classified into three types: constriction of the neck, suffocation, or submersion. On the other hand, due to pressure on the neck, we can have manual strangulation, strangulation by ligature, antebrachial strangulation, and hanging. By suffocation, we may have the occlusion of the respiratory orifices, the internal occlusion of the airways, by the chest and abdominal compression, by postural asphyxia, and the lack of breathable air.

Suffocation

Suffocation is caused by the absence of oxygenated air and by obstruction of its passage to the pulmonary alveoli. It is produced by obstructing the mouth or pharynx. Sharp, hyperflexion of the neck can occlude the pharynx, preventing air from entering the lungs. There are several types of suffocation: suffocation caused by confinement, chest compression, and obstruction of the breathing orifices. The suffocation can also occur due to airway obstruction, the cause of which is the glottis edema[7], choking[8], burial[9], and pulmonary aspiration[10] of foreign material.

Neck constriction

The asphyxiation caused by constriction of the neck is due to an obstruction to the passage of oxygenated blood to the brain. The situations that can lead to this type of asphyxiation are as follows: by hanging, strangulation, and choking. In the case of hanging, the neck is constricted by means of a loop in which the force acting is the weight of the victim's body. The characteristic signs of this type of asphyxia are the following: submandibular inverted "V" groove, modeled wounds of the loop, congestion above the level of constriction, tongue procidence, and hemorrhagic crest. The hanging can be classified in relation to the type of suspension of the body, so we can have the complete suspension (when there is no support from any part of the body) or incomplete suspension (when some part of the body is supported). Regarding the groove, we can classify it in relation to

- the number of laps: single, double, or multiple;
- the nature of the loop: hard (deep grooved, dehydrated, texture impression), soft (deep groove difficult to see), and mixed (groove with characteristics of the previous two);
- in the direction of the groove: ascending groove (knot at the nape, chin, or side), descending groove (when the head is in the lower plane), and horizontal groove (body almost in decubitus);
- regarding the neck perimeter: complete groove (across the perimeter, without interruption) and incomplete groove (not seen in some areas of the neck).

[7] Glottis edema—Glottis edema is a severe allergic reaction consisting of a sudden edema of this anatomical structure, which prevents the passage of air to the lungs. It can occur in the supraglottic region, retro arytenoid or subglottic.

[8] Choking—This type of suffocation due to airway obstruction occurs due to obstruction at the level of the laryngeal system, trachea or bronchi. This obstruction can occur due to food fragments and different foreign bodies.

[9] Burial—Consists of obstruction at the level of the bronchi and bronchioles, by small fragments such as sand, earth, cereals, etc. The victim's external habit shows fragments of the burial material. The victim's burial can occur due to falling earth or other components, which will penetrate the respiratory tract, causing asphyxiation. These cases are also referred to as submersion in solid media.

[10] Pulmonary aspiration—Consists of obstruction at the level of the pulmonary alveoli of gastric content, blood, etc. The external habit shows no external signs. The medicolegal etiology, in general, is accidental.

Examples of some types of suspension

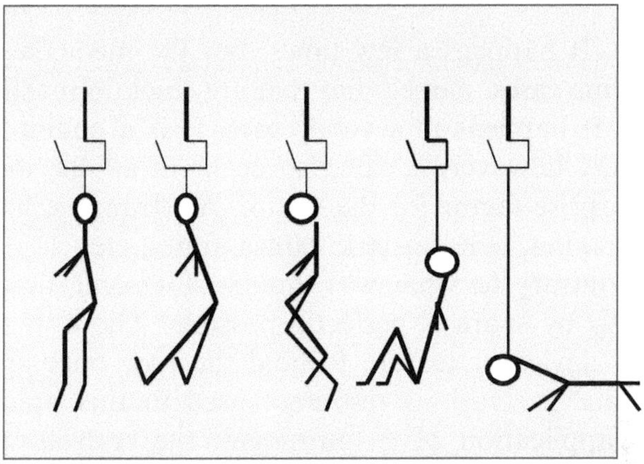

Picture 3 — Different types of suspension.

Strangulation

We call strangulation the violent death produced by a constriction of the neck through the application of an active force. Constriction can be done through a loop or the hands, giving rise to different injuries. Separate study of both varieties is mandatory, making it important for forensic nurses to have training on potential injuries and the risks associated with strangulation. Ligature strangulation uses an object to completely encircle the neck (e.g., hands, rope, belt), thus constricting blood flow to the brain as well as producing an airway obstruction. Ligature/restraint injuries often are accompanied by abrasions and contusions that occur at the injury site. Petechial hemorrhages also may be seen in association with ligature injuries.

In strangulation with a ligature, the neck is constricted with a force that is foreign to the weight of the body. The constricting force in the hanging generally acts in the direction of the body's axis while in the strangulation it is perpendicular to it. These are the essential differences with hanging, which must be distinguished from each other because both varieties of asphyxiation produce very similar injuries.

The medicolegal etiology of strangulation by ligature can obey a triple etiology:

1. Accidental—It happens a few times, but the medicolegal literature indicates some cases, namely ties that are stuck in machines.
2. Homicide—It happens in several cases. It is a common procedure in infanticide; however, it can also occur in adults, in this case, it can be a surprise factor for the victim. As strangles, handkerchiefs, towels, socks, ties, belts, electric cables, ropes, etc.
3. Suicide—Contrary to what was thought for some time, suicide by strangulation by snare is perfectly possible. The only thing that is needed is a device or feature to hold the bow once applied to the neck. Among the various resources used in this practice, can be found the application of a tourniquet, the realization of one or more knots, and the use of a belt that tightens in a ligature.

Manual strangulation

In strangulation by hand, death is caused by a predominantly asphyxic mechanism, with a neck constriction produced by the hand. Strangling by hand is exclusively criminal, since a person who compresses his own neck with his hands is unconscious, so it is very unlikely that suicide will occur in this way. Compression can be performed by either hand. The direction of the same takes place laterally with what closes the opening of the glottis in the anteroposterior direction, exerting pressure on the front part of the larynx. At other times, the compression takes place at a higher level on the hyoid, giving rise to a retropulsion of the base of the tongue closing the air passage.

The diagnosis of manual strangulation is based on the presence of marks on the ends of the fingers that cause asphyxia, which are investigated both on the surface of the neck and in the deep planes. The wounds produced by the nails are called nail stigmas. These cases are often associated with cases of sexual abuse and/or domestic violence. If the victim shows signs of strangulation, the medical team should exclude the possibility of sexual abuse.

Drowning deaths

In mechanical asphyxiation by submersion, death results from the penetration of water into the airways. The main sign is the presence of laryngo-tracheo-bronchial foam, which is characterized by a foam of fine bubbles, which are adherent to the mucosa, and which result from the mixture of water, mucus, and pulmonary surfactant. Submersion in freshwater causes death by ventricular fibrillation, due to electrolytic changes in the blood caused by water entering the lungs. In saltwater, death occurs due to pulmonary edema, since saltwater is a more concentrated solution than blood.

Submersion can also be by suicide, homicide, or accident. The fact that a body is found underwater or shows signs of having been immersed does not necessarily mean that the death resulted from submersion. Usually, submersion is accidental. In cases of homicide, it is frequent in situations of infanticide. Sometimes it is suicidal in nature and rarely conceals and simulates violent deaths. Examination of the scene and the body is essential. It is also important to know the position of the body and its relationship with the location. There may be indications that there was "ante mortem" submersion (in adults, retraction of the penis and nipples).

The most characteristic external sign is the foam mushroom in the mouth, as a result of the production of a foamy liquid in the lungs, which is then expelled through the larynx and usually appears around the mouth and nose. This foam is not found in bodies that have been in the water for a considerable time. When a body is recovered after a period of immersion, there are no outward signs to specify whether it was alive or dead when it entered the water. However, if the hands still hold fragments of another person's clothing or hair, this will raise suspicions of murder. Traumatic violence in life and abrasions on the forehead, knees, back of hands, and feet can also appear. Internally, the victim may have liquids and solid bodies in the respiratory and digestive tracts. There may also be congestion of the liver, dilution of blood and other fluids, ecchymosis of the muscles of the neck and chest, and pulmonary emphysema[11]. Usually, the victim has a dark head and swollen skin (like duck skin). The body may also present injuries caused by marine instruments, and/or marine fauna[12].

[11] Pulmonary surfactant is a complex of lipids and proteins capable of significantly reducing the surface tension inside the pulmonary alveoli, preventing them from collapsing during expiration. This lipoprotein complex is produced by type II pneumocytes of the alveoli and in its composition it has 80% phospholipids, 12% protein, and 8% neutral lipids.

[12] Nail stigmas—Excoriations due to the action of the nails, which can have a semilunar or linear shape when the nail slides on the skin.

Motor vehicle accident deaths

Motor vehicle accident deaths always raise the need for careful investigations, to ascertain the possible liability of third parties or factors inherent to the victim himself, who have contributed to the verified facts. There are multiple problems that can arise in these types of death, such as intoxication of the driver, human factors (speed, fatigue), environmental factors (degradation of roads, wet floor), and weather factors.

When fatal injuries result from an accident caused by a vehicle collision, overturning or colliding with the passenger compartment, the victims may be projected, either inside the car or outside, and it may be necessary to know what positions are occupied in the vehicle, namely to know who was the driver. A careful analysis of the traumatic injuries detected in the victims, and eventually their subsequent confrontation with the damage of the vehicle or vehicles involved, can allow a reconstruction very close to the reality of the facts [15]. Therefore the type of fractures, their exact location, the type of abrasions and bruises observed on the body surface should be noted. On the other hand, it is always necessary to investigate the possible influence of toxic substances (namely, alcohol and psychotropic substances), in triggering the accident.

Run over

Run over is the road accident most often causing bodily injury and death. It can be defined as the collision of a moving vehicle with a pedestrian (whether it is stationary or not). The factors that influence the characteristics of the injuries are as follows: the speed at which the vehicle is traveling, the type of vehicle, the fact that there was braking or not, and the height of the victim. Being run over has several stages [15]:

First phase—Clash with constant projection—The pawn can be hit frontally or tangentially. In either case, your relative position in relation to the vehicle can be from the front, the back, or from the side. When the impact is tangential, the kinetic energy[13] of which the vehicle

[13] Kinetic energy—A fundamental characteristic of the collision is that it takes place in a very short period of time in relation to human actions; in one or two tenths of a second a hit causes more serious and visible damage. Collisions are also closely linked to high speed, especially with regard to the damage they can cause. When speeds are high, the shock causes a set of forces

is animated is partially transmitted to the pedestrian, usually through a projecting part of it (mudguard, projecting side light). The victim usually spins on himself before falling. The injuries due to the fall are associated with those that are produced by the protrusions of the vehicle that hit the victim.

If the collision is frontal, the vehicle's kinetic energy is transmitted with greater impact and, of course, the injuries are more numerous and severe. In this case, the expert is usually asked to comment on the individual's position in relation to the vehicle at the time of the collision. The injuries resulting from the collision phase are, like those produced in other stages of being run over, of a blunt nature (abrasions, bruises, blunt wounds, fractures, dislocations). Some of them, however, due to their location and typicality, should be valued in the expert examination.

Fractures of the leg bones are common in victims of being run over. However, a tibial fracture is only characteristic of the impact phase of the bumper with the leg, if it has a cuneiform configuration. If the pawn is stopped (with both feet on the ground), bone fractures may appear on both legs. If the pedestrian is in motion, fractures of the leg bones arise in the limb that was lying on the floor. The lower limb, whether moving or not, has signs of fracture or when it does, it has an indirect fracture. At this stage, all the front structures of the vehicle are at stake. It should be noted, with regard to the radiator, the care that must be taken in observing the victim's clothes and skin, which are often thirsty for marks and modeled contusions where the structure in question is faithfully reproduced, of great medicolegal importance. When being run over by a rear impact by the car, the point of impact is on the legs, either above or below the knees, and the injury is caused by the bulges of the vehicle. Other injuries can occur, namely in the frontal region and the arms, since the body is projected forwards and towards the ground.

(acceleration/deceleration) so powerful that they exceed the limit values of rupture and integrity of the parts involved. But the human organism and tissues are much less resistant than the materials with which automobiles are built and this increases the risks for those who travel or for those hit by a moving vehicle. The "Kinetic Energy Theorem" relates variations in kinetic energy to the mechanical work that goes with it. Determining the speed of a vehicle involved in a traffic accident helps to demonstrate the dynamics of the event.

Second phase—Single fall or multiple constants—The fall phase, or better, of projection and fall, is due to the movement imprinted on the pedestrian's body. Depending on whether the vehicle speed is higher or lower, the projection can also take place over a greater or lesser distance. When the loss of balance is complete, the pawn, when falling, hits the ground, which can result in serious injuries. Some, such as those due to the impact of the skull with the ground, can be deadly.

Third phase—Dragging (fickle)—The victim is dragged across the ground, causing various injuries.

Fourth phase—Crushing (fickle)—This phase is not constant. Crushing is said to have occurred when the vehicle's wheelset passes over the body. Depending on the affected region, the following can be found: bilateral costal fractures and bilateral sacroiliac dislocation. The passage of tires over the victim's body can leave moderate bruises. The exhaust pipe or gases can cause burns. The lesions produced by entrainment are not specific, in many cases, there is extensive tearing of the skin and underlying tissues, without major hemorrhage.

Death by accident with motorcycle

The victims of accidents with the motorcycle are individuals of all ages, but with a greater incidence in the group of 16–17 years old. If a pedestrian is the victim of a motorcycle, the hit-and-run scheme is similar to that caused by a four-wheeled vehicle. As for the distribution of the wounds, we can see that the lower limbs are affected in the same proportion and there are small differences from right to left, as in the upper limbs. They are not usually fatal unless there are multiple fractures. Wounds in the abdomen and thorax require more care, as internal organs may be damaged. Those of greater severity are those of the head, which are almost always fatal [15].

Death by external physical agents

Burns

Burns are the most frequent accidents, occurring in a wide range of circumstances and at all ages. A 1996 study in the United States revealed an incidence of 4.7%, corresponding to 2.4% of trauma cases. The incidence in males is twice that of females, higher in children under 5 years old and adults between 25 and 34 years old. Most accidents occur at home or work. Two-thirds are due to hot or corrosive substances and a quarter is due to fire or flames. Although infrequent, of all disasters in which there are more than 20 deaths, 70% are classified as fires or explosions due to train crashes, airplane accidents, and underground disasters [19].

Burns can have different classifications. Thus there are four types of burns regarding their etiology: thermal (flames, boiling liquid, solar, ice), electric (high or low voltage), chemical (acids, bases), and radiation (nuclear, Rx). There is yet another classification of burns, which divides them into three categories, according to the distribution, the degree of the burn itself, and the existence or not of associated injuries.

The calculation of the burned skin area and the assessment of the depth of the wounds (first, second, and third degrees) are important. When we talk about degrees (first, second, third), we refer to the depth of the burnt area. However, the percentage of the burned area concerns the extent of the burned area. For this calculation, the 9% rule is used[14].

Deaths resulting from third-degree burns, whose skeleton, viscera, and cutaneous tissue have been charred, have the following general characteristics, without prejudice to other signs specific to the different types of burns: lower body volume due to complete cartilage carbonization and some fragments fragile bones, very hard touch, external wounds identical to those caused by the stab instruments, black in color, shortening of the legs and arms and the so-called "boxeur position" (due to the carbonization of the flexor and extensor muscles).

In heat deaths (burns), the Montalti sign corresponds to:

- hematic collection in the extradural space;
- boxer position of the carbonization victim;
- flictenas simulating putrefaction bubbles;
- presence of soot in the airways;
- disjunction of the skull bones simulating fracture.

[14] 9% rule—The 9% rule allows estimating the total burned body surface, according to the extent of the burn. In this case, we analyzed only the percentage of the body area affected by the injury, without considering its depth (its degrees). The rule of nine divides the adult's body into 12 regions: 11 of them are equivalent to 9% each; and the last (genital region) is equivalent to 1%.

Skeletal muscle contains two types of nerve fibers, whose function is to contract and relax. The first function is more potent and definitive due to the irreversible damage to the brain as responsible for the muscle action threshold. In the evaluation of chemical burns, in addition to calculating the extent of the burn, it is necessary to identify a possible inhalation injury and to suspect systemic toxicity. An example of this is the burn by hydrofluoric acid (common in the glass industry and present in the "clean rust"), which presents hypocalcemia and hypomagnesemia as a cause of death. Manifestations include hypotension, prolongation of the QT interval, ventricular arrhythmias, and consequent cardiac arrest [20].

Electrical burns

In electrical burns, it must be taken into account whether the burn occurred with high voltage (>1000 V) or low voltage[15], and whether it occurred with alternating current[16] or direct current. Between the two classes, the first is more dangerous, because it can cause tetanic contractions and serious bone and muscle injuries. Add that the heart is very sensitive to the alternating current of 60 cycles.

Electric burns can produce very serious internal injuries but on the outside, they are not very evident. It is important to observe the entrance and exit orifices, which are not always apparent on physical examination upon arrival at the hospital. Observing the victim on the scene, guided by the characteristics of the accident, is often the best way to identify burns. Among the causes of death by electrocution, we highlight the following: injury to the nervous system, respiratory arrest, interference with heart rhythm and contracture of the thoracic muscles, and asphyxia.

Lightning is another cause related to death by electric burn. The wounds that occur have the following characteristics: scorching of the hair, paralysis of the capillary vessels in the ray path (because blood is a good conductor of electricity and the vascular network increases the

[15] Low voltage—It is a term in electrical engineering used to identify the safety considerations of the system of generation, distribution and use of electrical energy based on the value of electrical voltage used. Despite the different voltage ranges used to define low voltage, it is generally characterized by carrying a substantial risk of electric shock, but a lower risk of electric arc in the air.

[16] Alternating current is a type of electric current whose direction varies over time, as opposed to direct current whose direction remains constant over time. The usual waveform on an AC power circuit is sinusoidal. As it is a more efficient way of transmitting energy, AC is usually the type of current that reaches homes.

effect), bone trauma generally occurs, due to the victim's projection to several meters away and a sudden increase in temperature up to 300°C, causing clothing to break and incrustations in the body by watches, rings or any meltable object. In the eyes, cataracts may appear which are a late but irreversible phenomenon.

Death by external toxic agents

Death by poisoning

Deaths from poisoning have often been attributed to suicide or accident, especially when the victim regularly uses drugs, on prescription, or to achieve stimulation. There are several types of poisoning/intoxication, however, the most frequent are CO poisoning, overdose, drug intoxication, and poisoning by pesticides and organophosphates.

CO poisoning—CO is a colorless, odorless gas produced by incomplete combustion of gasoline, diesel, kerosene, butane, propane, or coal. The symptoms translate into nausea and vomiting, followed by paralysis of movements, drowsiness, and death. The victims have discolored skin and pinkish pellets. The analysis for the detection of monoxide focuses on the blood, and there is no preestablished fatal level of CO. Heavy smokers can have CO levels of around 13% [21]. Children, small animals, and people who suffer from natural disease are more susceptible to CO poisoning. This type of intoxication should be suspected when more than one body is found on the scene and appears to have been a natural death. In most cases, the medicolegal etiology is suicide and accident. In the absence of fire, CO poisoning is usually attributed to accidental or intentional inhalation of car smoke and accidental or intentional inhalation of smoke produced by combustion of coal. The first priority of the investigation is the identification of the origin of the CO.

Drug intoxication—Drug intoxication occurs when drugs are administered in excessive doses, with a medicolegal etiology, accident, suicide, or homicide. In the case of accidents, they often result from inadvertent drug changes, incompatibility with other therapies, and administration errors. Suicide using drugs results essentially from the great ease with which they are acquired, the general knowledge of their actions, and the absence of physical violence. The drugs most frequently used are those with action on the central nervous system: hypnotics, sedatives, antidepressants, anxiolytics, and neuroleptics.

Pesticide poisoning—Pesticides[17] are substances used to destroy the fauna and flora that harms agriculture, being extremely toxic to the organism. With regard to medicolegal etiology, pesticide poisoning can be classified as: accidental, suicidal (large percentage), and homicidal (rare).

Intoxication by drugs of abuse—The drugs of abuse are chemical substances of natural, semisynthetic, or artificial origin, susceptible to consumption for nontherapeutic purposes. The most common are included in the following groups of substances: opiates, cocaine, cannabinoids, amphetamines, and other natural or laboratory synthesized products. Deaths of abuse drug users can be classified into deaths induced or directly due to drugs of abuse (overdose[18]), and deaths related to drug abuse (natural, violent, or undetermined cause) [22].

In situations where we do not find the product ingested or absorbed, we may suspect it, due to the symptoms that the person has. Therefore we now present some examples: rapid death, without special symptoms, suggests death by prussic acid or cyanide and potassium, with the body having a carmine color and possible smell of bitter almonds; dark-colored vomiting (like coffee), with the smell of onion and garlic, suggest the use of the deadly colorless phosphorus; Black vomiting and deep scabs in the absorption pathways, with a burnt appearance, with agonies of hours and days, are indicative of sulfuric acid; white vomiting, which turns black in daylight, suggests ingestion of silver salts, deep scabs in the yellow absorption pathways, resulting from the ingestion of etching (nitric acid); vomiting and diarrhea, abundant foam in the mouth, sweating and cramps are symptoms of absorption of mercury compounds, arsenic salts or lead.

Alcohol poisoning

Excessive alcohol consumption is identified as the fourth leading cause of death in Portugal, according to data from the World Health

[17] Pesticides are all substances or mixtures that aim to prevent, destroy, repel or mitigate any pest. A pesticide can be a chemical or a biological agent (such as a virus or bacteria) that is used against pests. It is used in several forms of living things, such as: insects, weed, mollusks, birds, mammals, fish, nematodes and microbes. They are not necessarily poisons; however, they are almost always toxic to humans.

[18] Overdose means an excessive amount or exposure to something, such as chemicals.

Organization. An alcohol-related death may be associated with short-term (accidental death) or long-term ingestion (effect of alcohol consumption, natural disease). Death is often associated with several causes since alcohol has a causal link with other diseases. In fact, alcohol is a poison. The person who drinks is protected from the effect of poison (alcohol) by detoxification (action) by the liver. However, all organs suffer from the chronic result of alcohol abuse, the result being associated with death from a natural cause.

The changes that occur in the organs are as follows: hemorrhages in the gastrointestinal tract, caused by a ruptured peptic ulcer, convulsive crises, with loss of respiratory function, disturbances of the heart rhythm, associated with malnutrition problems, and necrohemorrhagic pancreatitis. The primary focus of the investigation, in these cases, is on determining the mode of death and determining whether the death resulted from alcohol for the short or long term.

Sudden death

Sudden death in adults should always be considered, until proven otherwise, as a suspicious death, since it manifests itself suddenly or unexpectedly in an apparently healthy individual. In adults, the main cause of death is of cardiac and cerebrovascular origin, namely an aneurysm rupture. In these cases, it is extremely important to collect all the information that is available and that can help in establishing the cause of death. It will also be necessary to perform a complete autopsy, with the respective blood and urine collection for toxicology.

Observation of the scene is of particular importance in these cases, as we can find evidence that can help in the investigation of the case. Prehospital emergency teams must collect data on the victim's personal history, and properly document the maneuvers performed and therapy administered during the approach. In the study of a possible sudden death, one must answer two forensic questions: What is the cause of death: natural or violent? If violent, what is the medicolegal etiology (homicide, suicide, or accident)?

CHAPTER 6

Evidences with medical-legal relevance

Health professionals working in the prehospital emergency are the first to contact the victims, thus playing a key role in identifying, preserving, and collecting evidences. It is important therefore that they are aware of the priority that these evidences must represent in order to identify the circumstances that involved a certain fact. It is also important to be aware that everyone who handles the people in the place, where certain facts are verified, can leave evidences, change or remove them.

Understanding the importance of the evidence is the first step in learning how to maintain the evidence and not destroy it. Thus we can say that an evidence is everything we find in the place where the incident occurred or in the victim who, after being studied and interpreted by the experts, can turn into evidence, passing through the evidence phase. The vestiges, designated by Locard[1] [10] as "the silent witnesses to the crime," are therefore fundamental and the success of an investigation and a judicial process can often depend on them. This formulation structurally changed the attitude in the face of the construction of the criminal process: the new criminal investigator, armed with scientific reason, turned to the crime scene and looking for the footprint, the hair, the bloodstrain, and the fingerprints, started looking at the body, not only as if it were a body without a soul but, as an operative element that presents an informative potential, many times superior to the testimony and confrontations. In this way, the vestiges play a major role in clarifying the circumstances surrounding the event and the respective medico-legal etiology.

Evidence

The vestige may have individual or class characteristics. The individual characteristics reduce the vestige to a single common source

[1] Edmond Locard—One of the fundamental principles of the forensic area is the Locard Exchange Principle. According to this principle, anyone or anything that enters a crime scene takes something of the same with them and leaves something behind when they leave.

EMS in Crime Scene. DOI: https://doi.org/10.1016/B978-0-12-824420-3.00005-8

(an example of an individual characteristic is the fingerprints, unique to each person). Class characteristics reduce the vestige to a group (e.g., the fibers of a carpet can lead to the deduction that a particular carpet was made by a particular company) [23]. Vestige is the sign left by man, animal or object, which serves the investigation of an event, establishing particularities of its execution. It is therefore modifications/alterations resulting from human conduct, which allow drawing conclusions/interpretations. Note that the moment that a certain trace is related to the investigated event, it ceases to be a vestige and becomes known as evidence.

Evidence is any vestige directly related to the event, being a principle of proof of manifest. According to Malateste's theory [24], "after the occurrence of a crime, everything that is considered to be prior to it, is considered to be a cause of cause." Evidence, from a criminalistic point of view, is defined as any object material or information that is related to the occurrence of the crime. Therefore an evidence is the raw material found and/or collected at the scene of the incident, whereas the evidence is the evidence analyzed and debugged, becoming evidence by itself or together, to be used to clarify facts.

Courts recognize three types of evidence: direct, circumstantial, and real. Direct evidence is evidence that results from the testimony of witnesses. Circumstantial evidence is the physical evidence that establishes the circumstances that demonstrate the facts. The real evidence is that which proves, or not, the question under study [20].

Evidences in the context of the examination of the crime scene

Much has been written about the importance of the expert examination, considering it in its broad sense. Forensic examination of the crime scene involves a series of routines and procedures to be followed. Note that there are several categories of evidences, of which we highlight the following [25]:

1. True vestige—In the scope of an area where a crime has occurred, several elements will be left by the action of the offending agents. However, in this context, in the physical area, we will find many things besides the vestiges produced by the victim and the

aggressor. The true vestige is that which is produced directly by the perpetrators of the offense and also those that are a direct product of the action of the offense.

2. Illusory vestige—In this group, we find a greater variety of situations, in view of the countless possibilities and ways of producing the vestiges. The illusory vestige is any element found at the scene of the crime that is not related to the actions of the perpetrators of the offense and provided that its production did not occur intentionally. The production of illusory vestiges at the crime scene is very large, in view of the problem of the lack of isolation and preservation of the place. The main factors that contribute to the production of these traces are: people that transit through the place and the lack of knowledge of the techniques of preservation, on the part of the actors in the scene.
3. Forged vestige—The production of a forged evidence may prove to be very important to clarify certain circumstances of the crime. By forged trace, we mean all the element found at the crime scene, whose author intends to produce it, with the aim of modifying the set of original elements produced by the perpetrators of the offense. A forged evidence can be produced by anyone who is interested in modifying a crime scene, for several reasons.

The suitability of the vestige must be seen within a set of factors that range from direct actions by the experts in charge of the examinations, to the police officers present at that crime scene. The main door to safeguard the reputation is, without a doubt, in the procedures that the experts adopt for their verification, registration, identification, examinations, and analyzes necessary to arrive at the correct understanding of the meaning of each one of these evidences.

There are several stages in the collection and treatment of evidences, of which the following deserve mention:

- Finding—The expert search, at the scene of the occurrence, requires a whole methodology, to be adopted by the criminal experts, in order to guarantee the correct identification/visualization of the evidence, in the exact place where it is found. The finding therefore deals with the procedures, routines, and methodologies for finding evidences at the scene of the occurrence. In a superficial view, this task may even seem easy; however, experts know how difficult it is to find an evidence in certain situations.

- Registration—After finding an evidence at the scene, we move onto an extremely important second phase, which is the registration of the same, at the exact point where it was found and in the original conditions up to that moment. This register will comprise the detailed description of the evidence as it is found on the scene (photo, diagram, and drawing). All this concern with the registration of evidences in relation to the place aims to guarantee fundamental elements as to the certainty of the finding of that trace in that place, avoiding, thus that speculations and/or unfounded arguments arise about the existence or not of a certain trace, when someone is intent on privileging the information in the expert report.
- Identification—The identification of the various evidences found at the location of the occurrence requires some care by the experts, in order to guarantee the certainty of the object identified in later stages of the investigation.

Types of evidences

The evidences can be of different types, depending on their nature, presentation, and value. In this way, we can group the evidences into two major groups: the physical evidences (when they are materially individualizable) and the psychic or immaterial evidences (when they originate in behavioral changes). In this way, we can classify the physical evidences in: organic or biological, inorganic or nonbiological, and morphological. Biological evidences are identifiers and very common at the crime scene.

Biological evidences

- Fluids—Blood, semen, saliva, urine, secretions, vomiting, etc. These substances are analyzed serologically and biochemically to determine and identify the possible source and can be used for DNA analysis [26]. Blood stains and splashes of blood can reveal what happened to produce the bleeding. Blood analysis can indicate the type of drug, its levels present, and can also give an indication of the victim's position [27].
- Hair—Any human or animal hair that can link a person to the crime. Hair can also be used for DNA analysis.
- Physiological organs and fluids—Fluids are subjected to toxicology to detect the presence of drugs or poison [28].

- Bones/teeth—They can help with individual identification and are a good source of DNA.
- Nails—They can be used for DNA analysis. They are particularly interested in cases of sexual abuse.

Nonbiological vestiges

- Documents—Items that can determine the authenticity of the evidence.
- Medication—The presence or absence of illegal or prescription drugs.
- Explosives—All objects collected from the location of an explosion are suspected of containing explosive residue.
- Weapons and ammunition—Any intact weapon or ammunition fired can be tested and implicated in a criminal offense. The bullet can give an indication of the type of weapon used.
- Glass—Any particle of glass or fragment can be transferred to the person or object involved in the crime.
- Ink—Any ink can be transferred from the surface of one object to another.
- Dust particles—Any item suspected of containing gunpowder residues.
- Fiber—Any synthetic or natural fiber that has been transferred can be useful to establish a relationship between the person and the object.
- Soil and minerals—This evidence can link the person or object to a location.
- Wood and other vestiges of vegetation—Fragments discovered in clothing, shoes, or tools that can connect someone to the crime scene.
- Cigarette butt—It can be very useful for performing a serology test, helping to identify the smoker. It can also give an indication of the place of manufacture.
- Clothes—They can be an individual trait. The existence of dust residues from the gun can indicate the firing distance.

Morphological evidences

- Fingerprints—Individual identifications.

- Bite marks—They are often associated with crimes of a sexual nature, constituting good sources of information, to make the connection between the author and the victim.
- Lip impressions—They provide information on the link between the author, the victim, and the location.
- Instrument marks—Prints of objects used as tools in the context of crime.
- Footprints, footwear brands, and tires—They can be used to reconstruct the event, look for the author or the vehicle involved.

Particularities of some evidences

The firing residues present some peculiarities. Thus the short shot from the victim has a high concentration of smoke, vapors, and powder residues in the entrance wound. When the gun is fired, the waste is projected onto the target and is also on the person who fired it. Evidences of this residue are deposited on the back of the hands and can demonstrate whether the individual has recently fired a weapon [29]. The biggest difficulty with this type of evidence is the length of time that the residues remain in the hands. Residues are easily removed when washing or rubbing hands with a towel [30]. For this reason, placing paper bags in the hands of patients in the emergency room can help the investigation, so as not to lose the primary residues of gunpowder. If possible, venous access should not be inserted into the hands of patients with gunshot wounds. The use of paper bags is important and prevents the decomposition of the trace, which can occur if a plastic bag is used.

Methodology of collection and evidences analysis

In order to trace the evidence present at the crime scene, the expert must use a methodology specific to criminalistics. This methodology consists of the following steps: observation, description of the observed, collection of traces, and materialization of evidences.

Chain of custody

In order to be evaluated in the best conditions, the evidences must be well collected and preserved, using the latest techniques and technological equipment, which allow an improvement in their analysis and interpretation: "When collecting evidences, it is not enough to arrive at the crime scene and collect; an objective, integrated and studied approach must be made, enabling the collection and preservation of the remains in order to safeguard the information contained in them" [31].

The collection and sending of evidences requires that you have a permanent concern, so that you can later obtain the desired information. If the collection is not careful, following all the procedures, it can cause a deterioration of the evidences and loss of expert information. The process of collecting and preserving evidences must avoid possible contamination, as their occurrence may make it impossible to carry out forensic examinations to obtain the evidence [32].

The chain of custody is a procedure inherent to the collection of evidences and is an integral part of the scientific method of an investigation. To preserve evidences, preservation of the chain of custody must always be taken into account. The chain of custody is very important to avoid contamination of evidences [33]. According to Hoyos and Galindo [34], the fundamental characteristics of the chain of custody are as follows:

- ensure the correct identification of vestiges;
- preserve the vestiges collected, to avoid alteration;
- record all transfers and handling of vestiges, between the various actors;
- ensure that only authorized and registered people have access to the vestiges; and
- record all actions on specific forms.

In the chain of custody[2] registration, the following data must be filled in:

- Date/time and place of collection
- Identification of evidences
- Description of the evidences
- Identification of who handled it

When packaging the vestige, care must be taken that each evidence is in the appropriate container, and that the packages are sealed and

[2] Chain of custody—Chain of custody is understood to be the document where all the people that the trace has been registered are registered, specifying who handled it and on what date.

labeled. The vestiges must be placed in a primary container, which must then be placed in another, secondary one. All containers must be sealed. Hospitals should have a "standard document" for the chain of custody, which exists for the trace to be officially accepted in court.

Packaging and sending evidences

Evidences must be placed in suitable containers, which can guarantee their prescription and integrity, during the storage and shipping process. The sending of evidences must guarantee the maintenance of the chain of custody, and the identification of all persons and entities that handled the traces must be registered. When collecting evidences, individual protection must be used to avoid direct contact with them. It should therefore wear disposable gloves, mask, and gowns. You should not drink, eat, or smoke on the scene. It is also convenient to make a photographic record before collecting the evidences.

Proof

The proof is, in the legal definition and in a broad sense, the demonstration of the truth of the facts alleged in court. In the current sense, it is the appropriate means to demonstrate the truth of the facts, in terms of the whole, but also, in relation to each particular fact. In view of the way in which it is obtained or the means that produces it, the proof can be: direct (when it falls immediately on the facts, which are the object of the proof), indirect (when it falls on the diverse facts that, however, allow by means of rules of experience, and by logical reasoning, conclude which is the main fact).

Another classification makes it possible to distinguish between real proof and personal proof. Real proof is that which results from the observation of things, that is, it represents the facts to prove. On the other hand, personal proof results from the declaration of people, who report the facts as they saw it, learned it, or received information.

CHAPTER 7

Crime scene

The crime scene can be defined, generically, as a physical area where an unclear fact has occurred, which presents characteristics and/or configurations of a crime. [35]. More specifically, the crime scene is the entire physical space where the practice of a criminal offense occurred, therefore as a crime scene, any physical area that may be external, internal, or mixed is understood. This space is fundamental to satisfy the objective of the criminal investigation, which continues to be translated by the question: who did what? From the perspective of the scene, the investigator is required to define, albeit provisionally, a field of action, that is, it is necessary to collect certain information and adopt certain systematic behaviors.

As a rule, we can segment a crime scene into two parts: the physical component and the evidences. For example, even a place where a kidnaping, a rape, a homicide occurred, all the so-called evidence left by man, animal, or object serves to investigate the crime, because it establishes a particularity of its execution.

This importance results from a careful analysis of reality, since, from then on, materiality informs the way the criminal act took place, clarifies the motive of the crime, provides elements of the crime, allows its reconstruction, and helps in the interpretation of the most appropriate scientific methods. In terms of a good treatment of the evidences, it is necessary, immediately, to seal the scene and the accesses, to search in order to their identification, location, signs, and preservation and to proceed to the collection, conservation, and transport of the said, in the appropriate conditions.

The photographer is the first technician who works at the crime scene, with the aim of fixing the scene. Then, you must define the space, which involves acquiring an overview of the scene where you

EMS in Crime Scene. DOI: https://doi.org/10.1016/B978-0-12-824420-3.00009-5

will work. The reasons for the fixation by photograph[1] are diverse, namely, the changes that the place may have undergone by human action or as a result of atmospheric agents, or even due to the investigator's inexperience or failure.

These tasks allow, in subsequent analysis, the discovery of details that, on the scene, may go unnoticed. However, its main faculty will be to perpetuate reality and allow a subsequent reconstruction of the crime scene. As a general rule, nothing will be moved from the place without first being photographed, from a general, sectoral, and detailed perspective.

As for the techniques, regarding the execution of a search in a place, we consider the following: methodical and rigorous execution, knowing what you are looking for, locating all the evidences and proceeding to their signaling. This signage includes the marking of evidences on the ground, in chalk or through another indicator, as well as the placement of references (letters or numbers) and their fixation through position measurement, in relation to other (fixed) objects or walls. Regarding the samples collected, they can be of two types: of unknown origin and of known origin. For example, in the case of red spots, it is necessary to know whether they constitute blood or not. If yes, whether it is human or animal blood.

The tracks indicate that the bloody body has been moved from one place to another: if the body is dragged, the trail appears blurred; if the body is carried, drops of blood appear along the path. In terms of hair, they remain identifiable in a body long after the meat has been decomposed. Human hair are easily distinguishable from those of other animals, except for certain species of monkeys, and it is possible to distinguish clearly between hairs, depending on population affinities [36].

[1] Criminalistic photography—Photographic reporting of a crime scene is of extreme importance as it allows the location to be fixed exactly under the same conditions in which it was found at the arrival of the Judicial Inspection Team, both inside and in the near it. It also allows to fix, for later interpretation/valuation, all traces existing at the crime scene, whether visible or latent (using appropriate chemicals, forensic light sources and appropriate filters). Photographic reporting is an extremely important work tool that makes the examination report to the site much more explicit, allowing a better understanding/evaluation of the space and the facts that have occurred. Types of photography to be obtained from the site: aerial photography; general photography (ensuring, when possible, that any elements foreign to the site do not appear in it); composite (panoramic) photography; framing photography; and detail photography.

The crime scene has a unique and ephemeral character, which requires that the logic of the successive operations to be carried out be respected, and that a disciplined posture and correct acceptance of the method of action be assumed [36]. The main rules, in terms of behavior on the scene, which must be taken into account by the first element to arrive at the scene, include: approach and enter cautiously, obtain a global view, write down all secondary crime scenes, move away from the site unauthorized and nonessential people, preserve the scene without causing its contamination (involuntary and undesirable transfer of substances from one surface to another), protect evidences that may be lost or compromised (footprints, tire tracks), define and control the limits from the location, and record the victim's initial position or objects that have been removed, in the certainty that, in the meantime, nothing, at the crime scene, should have been changed [37]. The only exception to the rule will be the need to provide assistance to the victim or victims.

As for the criminal investigation team, it must have verified, with the element that initially arrived at the scene, all available information regarding the observations and activities, made by itself or by other elements, and then isolate/seal the surrounding area, to preserve any clue, approach the place (in order to prevent unforeseen situations or keep out curious people), absorb every detail, write down, and mention in the report any and all modifications produced on the scene, do not use the installed telephone, the bathing, taps, strictly controlling personal habits during the inspection (not smoking, not chewing gum, not eating, not drinking), not touching anything unnecessarily (not adjusting heating, air conditioning, windows, or doors) [38].

Establishing a safe area for the provisional storage of evidence and evidences is also essential, according to the chain of custody rules: stating the name or initials of the person who collected the evidence, the names of the people or entities to whom the evidence was transmitted, the date the objects were collected or sent, the name of the victim or suspect, and a brief description of the object [38,39].

At the same time, it is crucial to ensure that documentation is made that constitutes a detailed record of the crime scene, evidences collected and actions taken during the scene inspection, limit access to the crime scene to personnel directly involved in the inspection, use personal protective equipment to prevent personal contamination, and minimize contamination of the scene [38]. When technical conditions permit, the investigator should record volatile vestiges (smells, sounds) and record the time of departure from the scene, after equipment and materials used in the investigation have been removed.

Crime scene perimeter

The crime scene perimeter defines the size of the crime scene, and it is up to the investigator to decide how big the crime scene needs to be. The size of a crime scene is usually defined by the area where the criminal acts have taken place. This includes all areas where the suspect has had any interaction or activity within that scene, including points of entry and points of exit. The perimeter is also defined by areas where the interaction between the suspect and a victim took place. In some cases, where there is extended interaction between a suspect and a victim over time and that activity has happened over a distance or in several areas, the investigator may need to identify one large crime scene, or several smaller crime scene areas to set crime scene perimeters.

Assessment at the scene

There is normally only one opportunity to carry out an examination and recover relevant material from the scene of an offense or incident. It is vitally important therefore that all the possible evidential avenues at the scene are considered before any practical work commences. All relevant available information about the incident should be obtained before starting any examinations, and an agreement should be reached with the customer as to what is required to be ascertained. All possible hypotheses, from all sources, should be considered as part of this process.

The aim of the scene examination strategy should be to maximize recovery of forensic evidence and information from the scene within the parameters of the forensic strategy, existing policies and with due regard to cost effectiveness.

It is best if the scene can be preserved until all the experts are available. Where this is not possible or practicable, each scene examiner should ensure that adequate records are made of the scene prior to any disturbance of the scene on their part and during their subsequent examinations.

Scene preservation

All scenes, indoor, outdoor, or vehicles, should be protected at the earliest opportunity to reduce the risk of the loss of any material or post-incident movement or contamination.

Preservation of the crime scene is paramount and must be considered from the moment an incident is reported. The first contact officer and first responder have a responsibility to ensure the scene is preserved to the greatest possible extent to give the Scene of Crime Examiner(s) the maximum opportunity for forensic recovery.

All personnel attending the crime scene have a responsibility to ensure their actions do not compromise the recovery of forensic evidence. Scene preservation measures should include, as a minimum;

- Removal of nonessential personnel from the scene and subsequent controlled entry by means of a scene log.
- Cordons around the crime scene and other areas with potential forensic yield.
- Establishing and using a Common Approach Path.
- Wearing appropriate barrier (protective) clothing.

Measures are required to reduce the possibility of cross-contamination prior to the safe packaging of the materials at the crime scene. The minimum preventative measures include:

- The use of the correct protective clothing and disposable equipment should be changed when necessary during an examination.
- Equipment should be decontaminated after use.
- The effective management of the collection of different items in the same case for which connections are being sought.
- The use of different personnel for collecting material from the victim(s) and each suspect.
- When suspects are transported or interviewed ensure different vehicles, rooms, and officers are used.
- Having checks in place to ensure that recovered items, or materials obtained from them, cannot be mixed up with or transposed with other items or materials.
- The preventative measures required to avoid cross-contamination due to local environmental conditions.

- The principle that after material has been recovered, packaged, and sealed it must only be re-opened under controlled conditions and preferably not before laboratory examination.

Recording the crime scene

The crime scene should be accurately recorded prior to evidence recovery. The exception to this would be if there was a risk of losing evidence, for example, through inclement weather, while this process was being carried out. However, in this instance and if practicable, markers should be used to indicate where evidence has been recovered from.

The aim of recording the scene is to be able to clearly show the scene and any items within, for the following purposes:

- briefing authorized parties,
- evidential purposes,
- recording of any significant features of the scene,
- prior to examination and subsequent recovery of items, and
- recording of any significant items.

The methods used to record the crime scene can include:

- Still photography
- Video/digital recording
- 360 degrees imaging
- Plan drawing
- Taking of notes
- Any other suitable means: photogrammetry, lasergrammetry, etc.

The recording should be carried out in a methodical manner to ensure all areas are captured thoroughly and should be continued throughout the examination as necessary.

Recovery of forensic evidence from the crime scene

Recovered material should be handled as little as possible and packaged at the earliest opportunity. Control/reference materials must be kept strictly separate from any surfaces, items, clothing, or people with whom it might subsequently be significant to establish contact.

Consideration should be given to the following general points in the advice:

- identifying the right samples to take and how to ensure they are representative;
- the minimum amount of material required to obtain meaningful results for interpretative purposes;
- the amount and number of separate control samples required;
- guidance on methods for sampling that aid/assure the prevention of cross-contamination; and
- the need to preserve material for subsequent analysis by others (prosecution or defense).

CHAPTER 8

Criminal investigation

An investigation is a patient, step-by-step inquiry or observation, a careful examination, a recording of evidence, or a legal inquiry. The word investigate is derived from the Latin word *vestigare*, meaning to track or trace, a derivation easily related to police investigation.

A criminal investigation is the process of discovering, collecting, preparing, identifying, and presenting evidence to determine what happened and who is responsible.

Criminal investigation is a reconstructive process that uses deductive reasoning, a logical process in which a conclusion follows from specific facts. Based on specific pieces of evidence, investigators establish a proof, in that a suspect is guilty of an offense.

The criminal investigation comprises the set of steps that aim to ascertain the existence of a crime, determine the perpetrators, their responsibility, and discover and collect the evidences. In other words, the objective of the criminal investigation is translated by the question: WHO DID WHAT? [10]. The answer to this question is obedience to a methodology, based on rules of analysis, which are nothing more than procedures designed to find answers to so many other questions: Who? Where? When? What? With what? How? Why?

Who?

Not being the victim (body or not) recognized or being unrecognizable, the investigation uses elements such as fingerprints, signs or marks (congenital or acquired), garments, dental arches, bones, DNA, etc.

Where?

The examination of the crime scene is essential, because around it gravitate the evidences that, after being interpreted and correlated, allow the reconstruction of the circumstances in which the crime occurred,

EMS in Crime Scene. DOI: https://doi.org/10.1016/B978-0-12-824420-3.00015-0

possibly serving as evidence on which the fact-author relationship will be based. This first time is extremely complex, precarious, and fragile. Therefore it must be preserved and fixed until the arrival of the investigation team. However, it is not only at the scene of the crime that the perpetrator can leave evidences, but also in the access and escape areas, evidences of the criminal act can be detected: the smoked cigarette to calm down, the plastic gloves to avoid leaving fingerprints, etc.

When? (time—date/time/duration)

The determination of the time at which the fact occurred allows the concrete imputation of the crime, as well as restricting the number of suspects and assessing the veracity, or not, of the alibis presented. In terms of screening for homicide and suicide cases, the finding, reading, analysis, and correlation of late signs of death—temperature, livor mortis, rigor mortis—also allows the time of death to be determined with reasonable approximation.

The collection of information about the victim, namely the reconstruction of his last steps, is valuable for determining the time of death. For example, by combining the time when the victim was last seen, with the time taken to digest the food found in the stomach (calculated by the coroner when analyzing stomach contents), it is possible to get an approximate time of death.

In a car accident, for example, in which several people with children from different marriages die, the problem of succession lines arises, which forces us to find out who died before and after. Therefore there is no precision, but an approximation with a rather loose margin is made. When there is a high degree of decomposition, it is seen, for example, if there are larvae in the body, which may give an indication of the approximate date of death.

How? (modus operandi[1])

The degree of violence is closely related to the type of suspect and the motive for the crime. The modus operandi sometimes includes a set of acts or attitudes that are no longer necessary for the execution of the

[1] Modus operandi—Mode used to develop or accomplish something. Realization process. MO information can provide clues in numerous cases.

crime, which we call "signature." Its sole purpose is to provide the aggressor with personal satisfaction. Who has the intellectual and physical capacity needed to carry out a specific assault using a firearm, a stab, mechanical asphyxiation, or the administration of a toxic product?

When it is found that death is violent, the possibility of illness ruled out, the patterns of injury are essential to determine whether it was homicide or suicide. It is necessary to know how to interpret injuries and combine this work with on-scene examinations and criminal investigation. Such acts can occur before, during, or after the aggression, occurring frequently in crimes of a sexual nature and in situations of serial homicides, embodying a kind of "ritual."

What? (nature of the fact)

The position of the body is examined, the time of survival, what type of weapon was used, the sequence of injuries, and whether the body was moved or not.

With what? (instrument and means used)

The examination of the "external habit" and/or the autopsy provide data on the specific type of instrument used in the aggression. This determination restricts the number of suspects and, subsequently, allows the investigation to be guided in terms of carrying out steps to obtain evidence, for example, in searches.

Why?

The first clues, essential to the establishment of hypotheses about the reasons for the crime, result from the interpretation and correlation of the evidences found on the body and the surrounding scenario. It is this "all integrated" that allows you to rule out or admit a certain type of mobile, as well as to determine the existence—or not—of false evidences.

The incorrect interpretation of the evidences found, their inexistence, subtraction, addition, or concealment, can add to or irreparably compromise the investigation. Sometimes, the aggressor introduces evidences in the scene in order to evade the reasoning of the investigation, making one believe in the existence of another mobile. As a rule, this deliberate simulation occurs when the perpetrator premeditated the crime. As this situation requires mastery of the situation, it happens more in cases of victim/aggressor cohabitation.

On other occasions, in cases of accidental death by mechanical asphyxiation as a result of acts of autoeroticism or by hanging from a higher level person, the victim's family members, due to understandable shame or social prejudice, may "deliberately hide or remove" elements (cassettes, videos, pornographic magazines, etc.) that lead the investigator to assume a homicide or suicide when, in fact, it is an accidental situation. The detection of these situations can only be achieved after a sensible approach to family members and studying the victim's history. In some cases, there is also a negligent alteration, addition, or subtraction of evidences of the scene, as a result of untimely or deficient preservation of the scene, by family members, curious, and even police officers, even if they do not intend to evade the evidence.

The definition of the type of evidences to be detected results, therefore from the type of crime committed. A rape followed by homicide with a firearm requires that you look beyond the triggered capsules, biological evidences, hair, sperm, etc. The lack of evidences indicates that the author was subtracted, or points to the fact that the crime was committed elsewhere. In some cases, it denotes that there was no premeditation, the crime occurring in the course of another crime. For example, during a home theft, someone appeared inside the house, contrary to what the author assumed, and he panicked, committed a homicide, and immediately left the place without stealing anything. Not being the evident motive, only the psychological autopsy (retrospective and indirect exploration of personality and life) of the victim will make it possible to establish hypotheses about the reasons that in those circumstances of time, place, and manner could have led someone to commit murder).

Who? (author)

The timing of a suspect's hearing is only necessary when adequate, and sufficient evidence is gathered to connect him to the facts. As we know, confession unaccompanied by other evidence is worthless. In addition, the suspect is alerted and then released, either flees or completely destroys the evidence. The investigation must start from the evident to the hypothetical, from insurance to the uncertain. All the pieces of the puzzle must fit, and it is suspect A who must fit in set B and not any other.

The suspect always tries to understand the evidence that the police have already gathered, and the elements that the police do not yet know and will build an alibi on top of those gaps; therefore the suspect's intelligence should not be underestimated. Before starting the interrogation, methodical planning must be carried out, including the questions to be asked and their sequence. Questions should be asked clearly, in order to reconstruct the chronology of events. Sometimes, the investigator gets several answers to a question, and it is necessary to know how to overcome these eventualities. It is not convenient to ask questions whose answers are unknown, nor to immediately explore a contradiction between the answers and the evidence already obtained, which prevents the suspect from immediately correcting, from correcting what he said.

The goals of criminal investigation are to:

- Determine whether a crime has been committed
- Legally obtain information and evidence to identify the responsible person
- Arrest the suspect
- Recover stolen property
- Present the best possible case to the prosecutor

Crime scene

Successful investigation involves a balance between scientific knowledge acquired by study and experience, and the skills acquired by the artful application of learned techniques. The initial response is usually by a patrol officer assigned to the area where a crime has occurred. The initial response is crucial to the success of an investigation.

Communication

Without communication, there is no fundamental assumption for the beginning of the criminal investigation process: the notitia criminis. In the investigator's perspective, in addition to the knowledge he has of the punishable fact, it is necessary to define, even if provisionally, a field of action, that is, it is necessary to collect certain information and adopt certain systematic behaviors.

Type of crime

The type of crime register helps to refocus tasks in terms of skills. The criminal investigator must distinguish between criminal offenses and civil offenses. Even identifying facts that, in themselves, would constitute crimes, the truth is that given the verification of certain circumstances or qualities they will no longer be subject to criminal action.

Date/time

The time spaces (e.g., the time elapsed between communication and arrival at the scene) correlated with other known elements, bring precious indications to the investigation. It is not always possible to obtain the date/time of the crime in terms of communication. However, you should try to define, at least, the time space for its verification, since time, as an instrument of analysis, is often the guiding thread of the investigation.

Psychological autopsy

In the world of criminal investigation, namely in the field of determining suicide, the determining factor is invariably missing, that is, what was going on in the victim's mind at the time of death. In fact, a death should not be classified as a suicide until any other possibility that explains it has been ruled out.

Conceptual psychological autopsy is the retrospective and indirect exploration of the personality and life of an already deceased person. It is about making an assessment after death, of what the victim was like in life, being a kind of postmortem sociopsychological reconstruction.

Psychological autopsy as an expert technique appeared in the United States, only in the 1960s, as a way out of an administrative need that could define the medico-legal etiology of dubious deaths, for which there were not enough elements to say whether it was a suicide or an accident. This process, which begins right after the examination at the death scene itself in criminal cases, cannot be carried out only by an expert, but it needs the teamwork of criminalists, forensic doctors, and police investigators, because only then is it possible to achieve a deep and scientifically based characterization of the victim.

How then does a psychological autopsy take place within the context of criminal investigation? The main factor in this work is the process itself, the way of doing things, which starts from the actual place of the fact. Criminalistics experts can collect not only material evidences, but also psychological evidences, which are printed on the spaces the victim inhabited and on the people who interacted with her. For both cases, the death scene emits signals, which must be interpreted and decoded.

In this field, the victim's notes, diaries, letters, and other documents, which, despite not showing any apparent value, are essential for investigators, as the key is often among them, of the enigma of his death.

The second step is to interview people who have known the deceased, preferably family members, friends, neighbors, fellow students, work, religion, as well as formal or occasional close and mating relationships. It is important to clarify that the selection of information sources should exclude suspicions from people involved in the victim's death, as the risk of contamination is very high.

In this type of work, the possibility of intersecting criteria and hypotheses from the first hour between coroners, criminalists, and police investigators increases the effectiveness of this technique called psychological autopsy, as it allows enriching the scientific analysis of the victim and the circumstances surrounding death. Once all the elements necessary to obtain a characterization of the case have been collected, it is convenient to hold a collective discussion in which the experts and police investigators participate to enable expert information in probabilistic terms, as this is an indirect and the formulation of conclusions that only gain value in terms of the sum of the criminal, psychological, and medico-legal elements.

How to discern through psychological autopsy between suicide, homicide, and accident, in the context of a doubtful death, in which neither the coroner nor the investigator have enough elements to decide?

1. Valuing factors of suicidal risk, hetero-aggressive risk, or accidental risk
2. Valuing the deceased's lifestyle
3. Determining the mental state at the time of death
4. Establishing areas of conflict and motivation

5. Drawing the personality profile of the deceased
6. Determining whether there were presuicide warning signs
7. Determining whether there was a presuicidal state

Also as part of the criminal investigation, the psychological autopsy succeeds in establishing the circle of suspects in homicides of unknown perpetrators. By characterizing the victim with its conflicts, motivations, and lifestyle, forensic psychologists offer criminal investigators elements of probability as to possible perpetrators. In other words, not only the perpetrator and the victim are often suited to each other, as the living conditions of both often have complementary characteristics.

Local procedures

Criminalistics has its own methodology for the scientific development of its activities. Thus for work at the crime scene, a procedure consisting of a series of methodical, systematic, and chronological steps must be followed. Crime scene investigation is the point between science, logic, and law [10]. There is no typical crime scene, there are no typical evidences, and there is no typical investigative approach. The investigation of a location begins when the police receives the call. The system works like this:

1. The expert arrives at the scene and makes sure that it has been preserved. Then, it makes an initial recognition of the place, to check if someone has touched something before its arrival. The expert carefully documents the location, taking photographs, and drawing an outline, on a second reconnaissance. Sometimes, the documentation phase also includes a video recording.
2. The expert collects all possible evidences, labeling, registering, and packaging them, so that they remain intact until they reach the laboratory.

Recognition

When the expert arrives on the scene, he does not invade or start collecting traces. The objective of the recognition stage is to study what the investigation will entail and, in this way, develop a systematic approach to find and collect evidences. The first step is to define the extent of the location. It is very important to protect the site and other areas that may become part of the study. The protection of the scene implies the creation of a physical barrier and the removal of onlookers from the place. The expert can establish an off-site security area, where investigators can rest and talk about the case, without worrying about destroying evidences [37].

The expert follows a predetermined path, which appears to contain the least amount of evidences, which can be destroyed when walking. During the initial observation, the expert takes notes on details that could change over time: how is the weather? What time is it? Description of smells, sounds, anything that seems out of place or missing. This is the time to identify possible risks, such as gas leakage.

Body examination

The expert does at least a visual examination of the body and the surrounding area, taking pictures, and detailing the observations. Before moving the body, make notes of details: the existence of stains or marks on the clothes, the existence of clothes twisted in a certain direction (if positive it may indicate dragging), the existence of bruises, cuts or marks on the body, wounds caused when defending, lack of something (existence of sun marks, where there would be a watch or wedding ring), the presence of blood in large quantities (if the direction of flow follows the laws of gravity), the absence of blood in the area around the body (does this match the primary cause of death? If not, the body may have been moved), and the presence of blood[2] and other

[2] Analysis of blood stains—The main objectives of the analysis of blood stain patterns are to determine the events that originated the blood stain patterns and to reconstruct those same events, namely with regard to the movements of the actors, weapons, and hence blood. The definition of the directionality of the drops of blood is crucial, determining the point of convergence and area of origin of the referred stains, through methods that will be referenced and developed later on. As for the particular methodology of this analysis, the experts follow an already defined agenda: check whether it is actually blood and whether it is human (using blood identification tests); define, initially, whether it is a pattern of passive stains, splashes, or alterations; describe the types of patterns that are observed at the crime scene and where specifically; determine the possible mechanism that may have caused the patterns; decide if they have enough data to carry out the analysis with the software and if this is done. The analysis of blood stain patterns can be defined as the study of their shape, location, and distribution in order to determine the events that gave rise to them. These patterns can be created mainly by external or internal forces, through projection mechanisms by moving or transferring objects. Knowledge of the physical properties of blood described above is fundamental to infer the mechanisms by which the patterns observed at the crime scene were created.

body fluids. The expert must take fingerprints of the deceased and the location. Hands and feet must be covered with paper bags.

Examination of the scene

There are several investigation standards available to ensure complete coverage of the scene. These standards can include:

1. The investigation of the internal spiral type: the expert begins at the perimeter of the scene and works toward the center. The spiral pattern is a good method to use when there is only one investigator.
2. Investigation of the external spiral type: the expert starts at the center of the scene (or on the body) and works outward.
3. Parallel investigation: all members of the research team form a line, walk in a straight line, at the same speed, from one end to the other.
4. Grid-type investigation: these are two parallel investigations displaced by 90 degrees, carried out one after the other.
5. Zone-type investigation: the expert in charge divides the crime scene into sectors and each team member takes on a sector. Team members can then switch sectors and investigate again to ensure complete coverage.

Isolate the scene

One of the great and serious problems of forensics in places where crimes occur is, at times, the almost nonexistent concern of the authorities in isolating and adequately preserving a place of criminal offense, in order to guarantee the conditions to carry out an expert examination, the best way possible. When the crime is committed, the first agents to arrive are responsible for isolating the place and maintaining it as they found it. They must make sure that nobody touches anything, nobody moves anything, since, if they do, they are compromising the evidences or contaminating the scene. If there are still victims with signs of life, the police should call the EMS to assist the injured. The injured can be transferred to the hospital. The officer assigned to the scene takes care of the occurrence, the first few minutes being crucial to the investigation, as the agents will make preliminary observations and investigate the witnesses who were on the scene.

Scene protection

Securing the crime scene is a major responsibility of the first officers to arrive. Everything of a nonemergency nature is delayed until the scene is protected. The critical importance of securing the crime scene is better understood when one considers Locard's principle of exchange, a basic forensic theory that objects that come in contact with each other always transfer material, however minute, to each other. This evidence can easily be lost if the crime scene goes unprotected. At outdoor scenes, weather conditions such as heat, wind, rain, snow, or sleet can alter or destroy physical evidence. In addition, people may accidentally or intentionally disturb the scene. Additions to the scene can be as disconcerting to later investigation as the removal of evidence is.

The basic objective of protecting the crime scene is to preserve evidences that can be investigated and used in court. The evidence must be protected from intentional or accidental changes, from the moment it is discovered until the end of the investigation. Often, emergency medical teams are the first to arrive at the scene, so teams may be unaware that the incident for which they were requested results from a criminal act. While emergency care can be imperative, teams should approach the scene very carefully when a crime is suspected.

Sometimes, the potential aggressor is still in scene, so teams must pay close attention to their own safety because there have been several cases, where aggressions to medical teams have occurred. When teams are called to the place where a possible crime occurred, they must always bear in mind the possibility of preventing the loss of evidences.

There are two primary types of errors that damage crime scenes: commission errors and omission errors. Commission errors occur when a specific person or persons, be they witnesses, authority or medical teams, contaminate the place, in the most varied way (tracing evidences, messing up the scene, leaving cigarette butts, etc.). At any time, any person destroys evidences or adds evidences to the scene, thus causing a change in the site. The errors of omission, occur when the people who are in the place, do not transmit some important information, such as perfume odor, cigarette smoke, etc. These errors are in general not intentional but their omission can complicate the investigation.

The place where the criminal practices the crime is the carrier of criminal information. Timely and effective protection of the crime scene has the same value as sealing the treasury door, playing an extremely important role in understanding the core of criminal activities, collecting criminal evidence, discovering clues, seizing opportunities, excluding evidences or objects that they do not have nothing to do with the crime, improve the effectiveness and quality of the on-scene inspection, as well as, properly address the circumstances of the scene in order to prevent unexpected situations. The indiscriminate entry of subjects in the place does not only affect the validity of each of the evidences that can be obtained, as well as disturbing the concentration of those looking for other evidences. From the moment the information on the event is received, coordination with the police is an element of vital importance.

The procedures to be adopted are:

1. Putting barriers—A way to protect the crime scene is by placing ropes. The most common recommendation refers to the use of tapes and natural barriers. Tapes should be used at distances greater than 10 meters from the most distant evidence.
2. Rings—Since curiosity is an innate quality of the human being, every event that occurs outside of everyday life, draws the attention of the human being. The rings are used to establish security levels, control access, and keep people away. The rings are used in open scenarios. The main cause of contamination of the scenario is the police itself. Only specialized personnel should enter the scenario.
3. Vigilance—Remember that, more than a physical barrier, the police tape is a psychological barrier. A single point of entrance and exit should be sought. It is important to place a filter to control access, as this avoids the entrance of unnecessary personnel.
4. Physical barriers—These are those that, by their nature, prevent or hinder the passage of people. Inside, we have fences, windows, gates, and the like.
5. Checkpoint—The placement of several rings provides suitable places to establish a checkpoint, which has the function of serving as an operations center to organize the functions of each of the members or institutions involved. It is used in cases like airplane accidents, attacks with explosives or other disasters, involving the presence of different institutions, such as EMS/Red Cross/Firefighters, etc.

6. Eye inspection—Once the scene is protected, it is necessary to carry out an eye inspection, which aims to: assess possible dangers for the team or for the victims, give a vision of the event to redefine protection, establish priorities to carry out the work technician.

The area to be isolated, in cases of violent death, will comprise from the point where the body is (where the concentration of evidences is greater) to the limit where the last evidence that is visualized is found, in a first observation. This area will have an irregular shape, as it will depend on the disposition of the evidences and neither previous size nor spaces can be established. It will always depend on the visualization that the police make of the area, in order to observe as far as there may be traces. In places where violent death occurred, the visualization of some evidences, in certain cases, is not an easy task, given the variety and subtlety of these elements, present at the crime scene.

In situations where there are victims at the scene, the only thing to do is to check if the victim is really dead. From this observation, one should not touch the body anymore, avoiding a very common practice of touching the victim and his belongings, in order to establish his identification.

Motor vehicle accident death

The isolation and preservation of motor vehicle accident (MVA) scenes suffer from the deficiencies noted earlier. This type of occurrence must deserve all the care and attention for a correct expert examination. These places, by themselves, already present some natural difficulties (traffic flow, curiosity, traffic congestion), so, with accuracy, they are undone because they are impairing the fluidity of traffic or are at risk of other accidents.

Homicide

In the event of homicide, the examination of visible injuries is required, among other things. First of all, death must be confirmed, to detect situations of apparent death, resulting, in particular, from electrocution, drowning or ingestion of hypnotic products, and ascertain the motive of the crime, the modus operandi and the victim's curriculum. Signaling (phantom) must also be carried out, defining the position of the body, and note the exact positioning of the body in relation to the support surface, surrounding objects and fixed and immutable points.

At the same time, it is necessary to locate, photograph, and analyze all types of injuries/wounds detected, and note which is the probable instrument of the aggression.

The instrument has a special interest in two major criminal categories: homicide and assault. You can leave evidences, but there can also be vestiges on the instruments, and when you apprehend the suspect, you can decide an investigation. In the case of blood, the quantity and characteristics must be calculated, remembering that:

- blood does not clot in the body;
- bodies do not bleed;
- pools of blood can provide information on how long to survive.

Other crucial points are recording the existence of stings; protect the hands (e.g., in the event of a firearm being fired, to enable testing of paraffin[3] or Gonzalez's reagent); thoroughly examine clothing, to detect evidences of passive or active defense, namely as a result of fighting and/or aggression, or in the case of sexual crimes; record the probable time of death; if possible, take photographs properly framed to the body, in the original position, and in particular to the booklets.

[3] Paraffin test—For a preliminary answer, the collection of firing residues is carried out using a kit for detecting explosive substances (semicombustible particles of gunpowder that constitute the propelling charge of an ammunition). This method is merely an indicator, allowing the technician in a minimally satisfactory and swift manner, in situ, to assess the possibility of a certain subject having fired a firearm. It can be performed on living or dead people and various objects, such as articles of clothing, etc. For a definitive answer, the collection of shot residues is carried out with waste collection kits, consisting of an aluminum support with carbon adhesive tape mounted on a nonreusable watertight support, suitable for analysis by electronic microscopy. This is the mandatory procedure to collect residues from gunshots on living or dead people and objects (suspect's clothing, vehicle interiors, etc.), with the purpose of detecting the metallic particles derived from the deflagration of the primer existing in the fulminating capsule of an ammunition, performing the analysis by electronic microscopy.

CHAPTER 9

Intervention protocols

Of all that is exposed, it emphasizes the importance that the preservation of evidences will have for the possible resolution of a case. However, the emergency medical services (EMS) reality is far from perfect, since there is a great lack of training and knowledge on the part of doctors, paramedics, and nurses who work both in the prehospital and in the emergency department. All of this reinforces the need to propose procedures, within the scope of preservation, that is, the performance of protocols on the part of professionals working in the intra- and prehospital emergency.

As one of the objectives of this book is to become an orientation guide for health professionals, I propose the presentation of a standard of procedures for the preservation of evidences. Therefore I decided to divide them into two categories: preservation of evidences in a hospital environment and in a prehospital environment. I chose to expose the various situations that occur in the intra- and extrahospital context, as well as the procedures that must be performed to preserve evidences.

Emergency department

Evidences with forensic relevance are lost, in most cases, during the interval between the victim's initial injury and death, usually due to medical intervention or body displacement [40]. Preserving evidences is less complicated when a person dies at home or in a private place [40]. In a controlled place, teams ensure that important traces are not lost. When the victim is rescued, the vestiges become unstable and are moved in relation to the first victim's body. Within minutes, police, firefighters, and EMS arrive at the scene. Due to the large number of people who are in the place, the vestiges that can determine the circumstances that occurred before, during, and/or after the injuries or death can be lost, destroyed, or simply disappear.

EMS in Crime Scene. DOI: https://doi.org/10.1016/B978-0-12-824420-3.00013-7

The vestiges of victims who are transported to the hospital can also be lost. Medical teams, who are the first to contact victims, should be trained to recognize, collect, and transmit biological evidences [40]. Emergency care is the top priority for emergency teams and should not be delayed for collection of documents or preservation of evidences on scene. Victims who are transported by the helicopter are the most complicated to preserve evidences [20].

The collection of evidences in emergency department requires basic individual protection care to avoid contamination. Thus for the collection of evidences, the following protective equipment must be worn: gown, gloves, mask, and cap. Gloves should also be changed whenever different evidences are collected. It is always necessary to pay attention to the adequate storage of the evidences and the proper sending of them to the laboratory. Accurately, doubts arise about a certain item, if it can be considered as evidence, when in doubt, carefully collect and preserve it [20].

All evidences must be packed separately. Items, wet or steamed, must be dried in the open, before packaging. Wet items should not be placed in plastic bags, always using paper bags or containers with respirators. The vestige should never be left unsafe or unattended. All bags with vestige and containers must be closed, with a resistant lid and labels with the name of the patient, number of emergency episodes, date, time of collection, and name of the person who collected the items, thus maintaining the chain of custody [20].

Basic care

Taking care of the body is the responsibility of the medical team. In this sense, the venous accesses and the tubes placed during resuscitation must remain intact, after resuscitation ends [41]. You must clamp or close the intravenous lines and then cut to small size [41]. The chest drains must be disconnected from the drain bottles, clamped, and left in place [41]. The catheters are disconnected from the drainage bags and are clamped, remaining in place [41]. All venous punctures must be marked with a circle (permanent ink) to allow the distinction between venopunctions and preexisting puncture wounds [41]. The organs and parts of the body that have been removed during resuscitation must be placed in containers, labeled, and sent, with the body, to the morgue.

To summarize the procedures for preserving and collecting evidences, teams should follow the following recommendations [20]:

- always wear gloves and other protective equipment (gown, mask, cap);
- change gloves frequently to avoid cross contamination;
- clothing and personal belongings should not be given to family or friends;
- put each evidence in a separate bag and identify it with the victim's name, name of the person who collected it, date, time, and content;
- dry all specimens before packing;
- bags/envelopes/containers must be sealed and an identification label must be attached;
- do not staple the bags to close;
- document everything and sign;
- all victims of violent death must be completely stripped and their entire body be examined.

Collection of body fluids

In the emergency department, it is common practice to collect blood into several tubes. In the case of forensic victims, blood should be collected into two tubes (dry tubes), which must be kept in a safe area. If the patient dies, blood test should be requested as they contain the values before transfusions and drugs have been administered, as well as the cases in which hemodilution occurs by the crystalloids used during resuscitation [20]. If there are bloodstains on the body surface, the following steps must be completed:

1. Nondried blood or other substances—absorb the material with a dry swab, let it dry, and then place it in an envelope. Do not use plastic containers.
2. Dried blood—it must be collected with a moistened swab, with two drops of sterile water. After collection, let it air dry and then store in an envelope.

To collect gastric or urine content, use sterile containers. If there is vomiting on the floor, a tissue should be used to absorb the fluid. After absorption with the towel, it should be allowed to air dry and then put in an envelope. If it is not possible to dry the towel well, it should be placed in the envelope, and the envelope should be placed in a plastic bag or glass bottle. Other evidences, such as semen or other fluids, can be collected in the same way, using dry swabs or moistened with distilled water, depending on the state of the evidence [20].

Invasive techniques during resuscitation

In cases where a violent death has occurred, the body must not be explored, altered, or taken away. Obviously, objects that are impaled on the body should not be removed. When resuscitation is unsuccessful, if there are bullets, try not to remove them from the wounds. Wounds caused by bladed and firearms should not be explored during resuscitation unless it is really necessary for the victim's survival [42].

Chest drains should not be placed on existing wounds, and the doctor should avoid making incisions at existing wound sites, and if he does, this information should be placed in the notes. In trauma victims, paper bags should be placed in their hands to try to preserve any evidences that may exist on their hands and under their nails.

Spoils

A victim's estate is a vestige. All clothing and material removed from the victim must be placed and stored in appropriate bags and sealed with the victim's identification [43]. Care must be taken not to lose anything or damage clothing. If the police do not receive the clothing immediately, the hospital must make a list of supplies to be handed over to the police [43]. Whoever removes the victim's estate must document the fact and discriminate the content. Often, in cases of traumatic death, the identification of the deceased is not easy to establish, so one should only use the name "Unknown male/female."

Clothing

Clothing can contain vital information, which can translate into evidences or corroborate the victim's story. It is important that the clothing is treated with attention and care to avoid contamination or loss of important evidences. When the patient enters the emergency department, the priority is to save the person's life, and only afterward the preservation and collection of evidence. For this reason, clothing is sometimes neglected. In some cases, it is possible for victims to take their own clothes, in which case, victims should be instructed to take their clothes off on a white sheet.

After storing the clothes, make sure that the sheet is also stored so that all evidences are collected. To simplify the removal of the victim's clothing, some professionals cut the clothing through the existing holes. Sometimes, these holes were caused by penetrating objects (bladed weapons, firearms). It is extremely important that these holes remain intact so that the Scientific Police Laboratory (SPL)[1] can use the suit for investigation. The ideal is to undress and, if necessary, cut it at the seams. After removing the clothes, do not shake as traces may be lost. The clothes must be stored dry, and one piece should be placed in each paper bag [20].

Plastic bags are not recommended as they can deteriorate certain evidences, especially biological evidences, such as blood and other body fluids. Clothes should be dried outdoors before storing. In case it is not possible to dry the clothes, they should be stored in plastic bags, using paper on top of the wet areas, and always bearing in mind that the bags should not be closed. You must put the pieces in separate bags and inform the police that the traces are wet. Staples should not be used to seal the envelope, which can pose a potential risk of injury to the person handling it [44]. "Clothing" must be indicated on the envelope label. If the patient is brought in by ambulance, the sheets of the ambulance must be kept. Shoes can be a very important vestiges, therefore one shoe should be placed in each bag.

Often, clothing will be wet from body fluids such as blood. If at all possible, air dry the clothes in a secure location. If you do not have the facilities to air dry the clothing, package them with clean paper between the wet stains (to avoid cross contamination), place them in individual paper bags, and inform the police officer collecting the evidence.

[1] SPL—Scientific Police Laboratory—has the following competences: (1) investigate, collect, treat, record evidences, and perform expertise in the various fields of forensic sciences, namely ballistics, biology, documents, handwriting, physics, lofoscopy, chemistry, and toxicology; (2) implement new types of expertise and develop existing ones; (3) disseminate technical and scientific information that is relevant to new crime scenarios; (4) issue opinions and provide technical and scientific advice in the field of its competencies in forensic sciences; (5) implement a management system for quality and for administrative and technical activities; (6) ensure the technical and scientific participation of the criminal police, in matters of forensic sciences, in the different national, community, and international bodies.

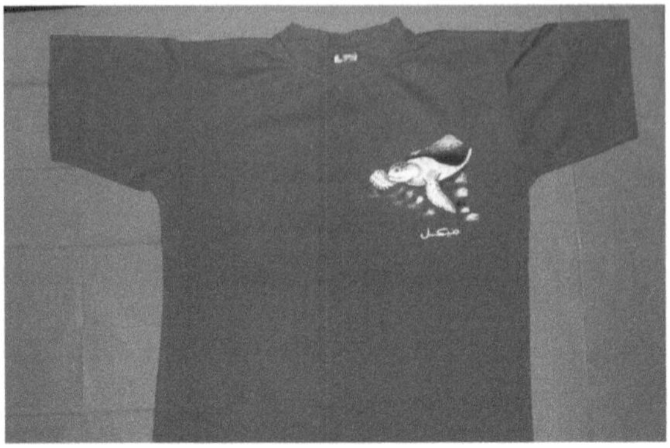

Picture 1 — Preparing clothes for packing.

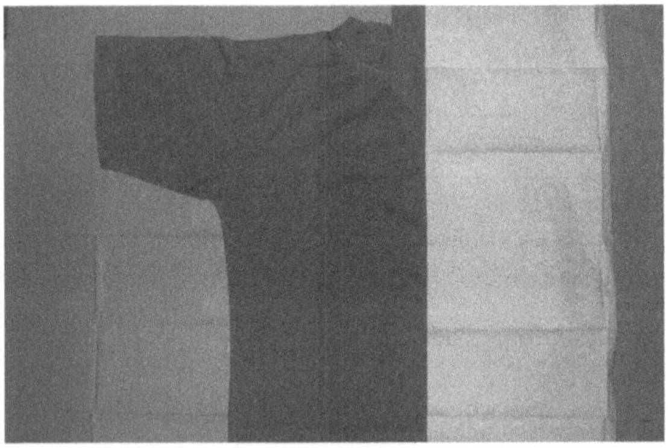

Picture 2 — Preparing clothes for packing.

Picture 3 — Preparing clothes for packing.

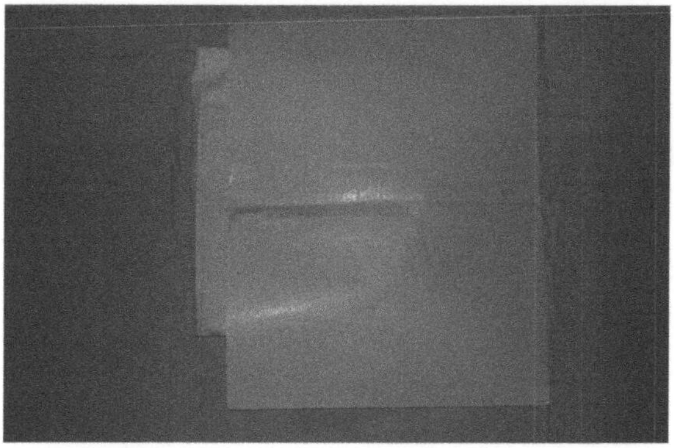

Picture 4 — After finishing put inside envelope and seal.

Weapons

The weapons removed from the victims must be given to the police, if it is not present, and must be given to the security of the emergency department. Bullets removed during treatment must be preserved and must be documented in the clinical process. Care must be taken not to damage the bullet. As such, tweezers with rat teeth should not be used [44]. Preferably, clamps, coated with rubber, should be used.

Even the bullets that are damaged must be sent to the SPL. The bullet must never be marked by the medical team and must not be cleaned (do not remove blood or fragments) [20]. After the bullet is removed from the body, it will be placed in a candy box (urine collection container), which can be replaced by a paper envelope [20]. This envelope must be identified with the time, date, medical team, and the location from which the bullet was removed, all this information must be documented in the clinical file. If there are several bullets, each must be placed in separate envelopes, numbered in order of removal, and containing relevant information.

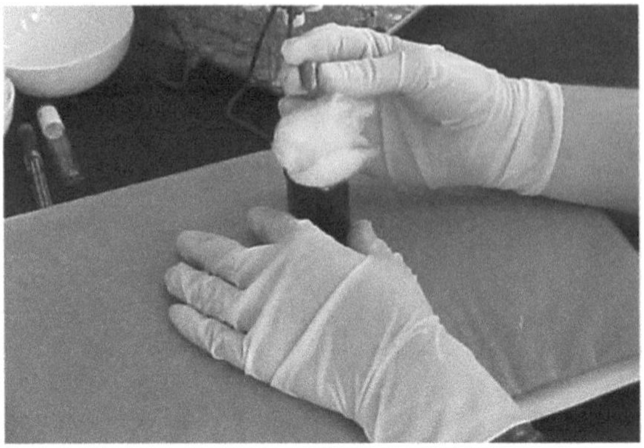

Picture 5—Placing cotton in a urine collection container.

Health professionals should not speculate about what happened in relation to injuries. The entrance wounds and exit wounds of the bullets are sometimes obvious. However, it should not be generalized, since self-inflicted wounds on the head can present an entrance wound larger than the exit wound. If a camera is available, some images of the wounds should be taken before destroying the evidences. If there is no camera, the description of what the wounds look like should be documented prior to their exploration (exploration should only happen if it is really necessary).

It is also important to place large items, (such as knives and weapons), in boxes of appropriate size, covering the box with gauze or cotton, to protect the items, and handle with great care, locking the gun with improvised blocks (pills, catheters) veins, pen caps, etc.). Here are some examples of weapon blocks.

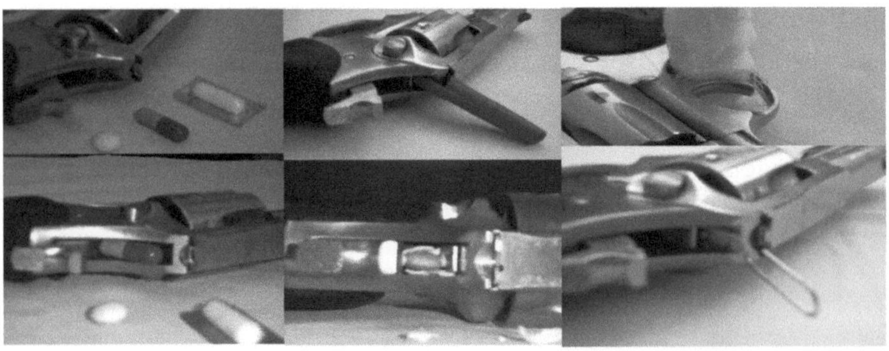

Picture 6 — Block gun for safety. Can be used several objects.

Picture 7 — Blocked gun with venous catheter.

Penetrating missiles

Occasionally, you will handle penetrating missiles (i.e., bullets) in the emergency department (ED). There are some important points to remember in regard to retrieval and collection of any penetrating missile. Use sterile gloves or a rubber-tipped forceps to retrieve the missile. If rubber-tipped forceps are not available, use regular forceps protected with gauze to prevent any unintentional tool markings or indentations that might interfere with ballistic tests. Place the missile in a sterile container, padded with gauze to protect it. Use great care to avoid scratches or indentations. Even slight indentations can make a ballistics match impossible. Proper labeling of the container should be done promptly and the chain of custody ensured.

Other objects

Hair, fibers, glass, paint, or other unknown materials may be on the clothing and must be placed in the container using the correct procedures. Small glass fragments, as well as other types of fragments, must be stored in test tubes [45].

Bite marks

The marks of a bite can be evidence in a lawsuit since they have individualizing characteristics such as a fingerprint. As a result of sexual assaults, bites may appear, combined with signs of sucking, producing a red mark, with a central stain and peripheral ring. In nonsexual assaults, the teeth are used as weapons and the bite is strong and fast, with no red mark. It is essential to take samples from the site before the molds are made, as the residual saliva can be used for blood group determination or for DNA analysis. Therefore swabs should be performed around the bite. If the skin is dry, moisten the swab with distilled water, but if the skin is moist, use dry swab. If possible, it is important to photograph the bite mark and make a detailed description of it in the clinical process.

Examination

Patients with injuries of any type should be completely undressed and all body surfaces inspected. Often a seemingly minor wound on a hand, arm, leg, or face may be accompanied by fall more serious indications of trauma on the chest, abdomen, or back.

Examination requires complete inspection of all body surfaces and parts, including genitals. The examination procedures must be done with great care to prevent further pain, fear, and embarrassment. At the same time, note the patient's behavior and reactions to your examination. It is considered good practice to conduct the examination and assessment with another nurse or physician because they confirm your findings and your account of the examination.

Healthcare personnel should be able to detect injuries with patterns not ordinarily associated with accidental trauma. Statements such as "the child fell down the stairs," "he fell out of bed," "his sister hit him," "I was asleep when it happened," etc. should raise your level of suspicion.

Usually, a thorough examination, documentation, and photographs will help to support or refute the story about the injuries and the associated events.

When interviewing and examining patients, be certain to note any key indicators of abuse. Some of them are as follows:

- unexplained or unwitnessed traumatic injuries;
- delays in seeking medical care postinjury. The general pattern seems to be delay in seeking treatment until the morning after or several days later. The caregivers or spouse are then likely to exhibit indifference to treatment, prognosis, and the patient in general;
- multiple injuries, clustered and on different body surfaces. Example: soft-tissue swelling on one shoulder with several bruises on the opposite anterior chest wall. (Document the location, size, shape, and color of bruises);

- multiple similarly shaped lesions in various stages of healing. Example: two fresh and weeping, two crusty and pustular, and one dry with pink edges and dark center (e.g., insect bites, intentional burns);
- injuries that reflect the outline of an object or mode of infliction. Examples: handprints, belt buckles, looped electrical cords, curling irons;
- injuries inconsistent with the account of the accident or explanation of cause that is implausible. Example: A 9-month-old child "climbed" into a bathtub of hot water and burns were clearly outlined 1 inch above both ankles;
- suspiciousness that the injury has been intentionally produced.

Other considerations

If there are apparent gunpowder residues in the victim's hands, paper bags should be placed in the hands and sealed with adhesive. In parallel, the victim should be punctured in central locations and never on the back of the hands. In situations where a victim already is DOA (death on arrive) in an emergency or dies in the emergency room, the following procedures should be followed to ensure that no evidences are lost: protect the emergency room and contact the police (in cases where there is suspected violent death), do not wash the body, and do not remove venous accesses, tubes [46].

Vials of medication, fluids, drugs, and invasive material that have been used for resuscitation should be kept and urine, gastric contents, and chest drainage contents should be collected, until it can be measured, examined, and preserved. It is especially important, in cases of intoxication or overdose, the collection of medication, drugs, and toxics that are with the victim. It should also be noted the importance of drawing a circle with a skin marker in places where there were venipunctures and drains. If incisions are made during treatment, it should be recorded in the notes of the clinical file to ensure that the wounds are not confused with the trauma that occurred in the prehospital.

Family members or other visitors should not touch or move the body, due to the possibility of destruction and contamination of the remains. Health professionals themselves should not touch the body, except for those who started the process of collecting evidences. The body must be wrapped in a sheet before being placed in the bag, so that evidences are preserved and that they are not transferred to the bag. The body must be identified with three labels: one on the upper limb, another on the lower limb, and another on the chest, before being transferred to the morgue.

Prehospital

In a prehospital environment, one of the specificities that occur is the fact that teams are faced with situations of risk and violence. When EMS are called to potential violent locations, they must request the presence of the police. The immediate recognition that a location may be violent requires a high level of attention and suspicion. It is therefore essential to analyze the situation and intervene only if there are security conditions. In this approach, the following aspects must always be respected:

- do not approach the scene without it being safe;
- pay particular attention to places that present potential risks;
- approach the location, using the route that is the safest and not the easiest;
- monitor access to the scene before approaching the victim;
- keep unnecessary people away from the victim;
- do not start unnecessary conversations with witnesses, respect the present police, and the instructions given by it.

When EMS are called to violent scenes, it is best to remain in direct radio contact with the 911 center. This attitude allows the team to receive information about the location, security issues, and the presumed number of victims. There is a standard rule at the crime scene "Do not touch anything"—this warning is not an option for emergency teams, since the action protocols indicate that they must control the bleeding, intubate, defibrillate, perform CPR, immobilize, and transport the victims to the hospital. Therefore "Do not touch anything" is impossible.

If advanced life support maneuvers are performed (with endotracheal intubation), it should be documented, since artifacts can be created that can create problems for the investigation teams. These artifacts are associated in the case of orotracheal intubation in possible trauma that can occur in the oral region and that can lead to the suspicion of aggression (broken teeth, contusions of the mouth and lips). On the other hand, external cardiac compression can lead to fractures of the ribs, sternum, and cardiac trauma, which in the context of medicolegal autopsy can lead to conclusions of potential aggression. These artifacts will be covered in another chapter.

EMS have as a top priority emergency care to the victim, making the recognition and preservation of vestiges secondary actions. However, teams that have training in the forensic area automatically integrate the preservation of evidences in their practice, without neglecting medical assistance. Whenever EMS have activations for calls where there is a suspicion that the victim may have already died, they must take the following measures:

1. park the ambulance outside the braking marks or other traces (if it is a motor vehicle accident (MVA));
2. always enter and leave the same place;
3. document everything that happens around the victim and the location (attention to odors and noises);
4. the paramedic document form must include: activation time, arrival at the scene, time of death, places of entrance and exit, changes made to the scene by the teams (moving furniture, body, etc.);
5. describe the actions taken on the scene (resuscitation maneuvers);
6. the disposable equipment used on the victim must be left on the scene;
7. gloves or other material used must be placed in paper bags, closed, and left in scene.

Crime scene procedures

It is common for the EMS to arrive at the scene first than the police, and in such situations, they must determine the safety of the scene. In case of no such, the team must inform the 911 center and wait for the police to arrive [47]. At the scene of the crime, EMS will follow the platinum rule "10 minutes on the scene."

When teams are called to potential hazardous locations, they must use appropriate sound and visual signals. However, in urban locations, the excessive use of sound signaling can draw people's attention, and as such, lead to the presence of crowds. Visual signage is generally indicated for safety and signage issues on the scene. If possible, it is important to combine visual signals between firefighters and EMS to identify the location. Even after the place is guaranteed to be safe, teams must pay attention to the place. In fact, a scene that at first appears to be safe can be unsafe at any time, even in the presence of police at the scene.

The approach to a hazardous residence requires a lot of attention and care for the following aspects:

1. history of violence problems;
2. zone known for the presence of drugs or gangs;
3. abnormal noise (screams, shots, objects to be thrown);
4. see or listen to acts of violence;
5. the presence of alcohol and drugs;
6. the presence of dangerous animals;
7. suspicious silence, in an area that is usually busy.

If any of these warning signs are present at the scene, the EMS must leave the scene and request police assistance. When approaching a suspicious residence, the medical team must take some measures, such as avoid using sirens, avoid standing between the ambulance lights and the residence. The medical team must also listen to the warning signs before announcing their arrival and before entering the home [48], and when moving to the residence, if using a flashlight, use it next to the body, to be lit from a distance. It is also important to try to walk on grass to reduce noise. The two elements must walk in a single file, the first element carrying the flashlight and the monitor, and the second carrying the medical bag and the resuscitation bag.

EMS should avoid being in poorly lit areas, where only shadows can be seen, because an attacker who is disoriented can become quite aggressive and, if armed, could put health professionals at risk. If they suspect violence, teams must put themselves in a guarded position and wait for the police to arrive. Likewise, if they suspect shooting, they must remain in a protected place.

The EMS should approach doors and windows from the side and never from the front and should never stand facing the door when knocking or ringing the doorbell. After opening the door, the team must stand 2–3 m away, with the medical bag or the cardiac monitor in front of the body, so it can be used as a means of defense. The team must identify itself, who is already on the scene [20]. In the event of an aggressive situation on the part of family members, support from the police should be requested whenever necessary. When entering the scene, care must be taken not to destroy the evidences. However, one should always be aware that caring for the victim is always first. When it is necessary to enter the crime scene, the team must be attentive to the noise of the scene, as well as make a mental map of the patient's location, the presence of blood, weapons, and other items, which are outside the scene, or anything that seems important.

Picture 8 — Approaching the door. stand aside and announce arrival and identify.

Picture 9 — Do not approach doors from the front, the exposure of the element can be dangerous.

Picture 10 — Put it aside, knock on the door and identify.

Picture 11 — Opening the front door leads to high dangers.

Picture 12 — In front of an armed person the EMS exposure is total.

Sometimes, to access the victim, it may be necessary to move furniture. When this happens, you must memorize their original location, as well as the moved evidences, for later description. On the scene, security is easy and in many cases, you just need to close the door. When standing next to the victim, misunderstandings that may disturb the victim or the place where he is located should not be allowed.

The team must remain in control, because carrying out their actions in an almost chaotic scenario can become an impossible mission. Remember that if we do not control the scene, the scene will control us, and we must maintain the notion that the size of the site is a dynamic process and that it can become dangerous after we initially thought it would be safe. In case of facing groups or flocks, the leader of the group should be checked quickly to enter into dialog with him. If a violent situation is suspected, you should ask for reinforcements.

Observing the body language of the people who are in the place is essential. In fact, an aggressive posture, with feet apart, hands on hips, arms crossed, and stare, with physical innuendo, are some warning signs. Some techniques to avoid physical violence are as follows:

- throw equipment (light bags) at the aggressor;
- put the door on the stretcher;
- use an unconventional path to retreat;
- anticipate the aggressor's movements;
- drop objects in the aggressor's path;
- use preprogrammed escape techniques.

Picture 13 — In front of a person in an aggressive position and with object in hand take safety measures.

There are also some anti-violence tactics, which consist of the team retreating through an emergency exit, protecting themselves behind solid objects, using distraction and escape, with defensive movements, and transmitting warning and radio communication signals. The teams must adopt communication and alarm techniques among themselves, so as not to be recognized by the aggressor. You can, for example, use the code, Echo Mike. In situations of risk, it is possible to communicate with the 911 Call Center, without direct contact (share the radio for the 911 Call Center to hear).

EMS should take a cautious approach, speaking with a firm and calm voice, explaining the team's role and the procedures that will be performed, calming agitated people, and, if necessary, considering the use of drugs. In particular, in cases involving ethnic minorities, the rules of the ethnicity concerned must be respected when approaching the victim and the situation, and a reference person should be involved in the approach.

Communication

One of the most important aspects of interaction at the crime scene is communication between all personnel working on the scene. In effect, police and EMS must communicate about the actions and observations of the personnel on scene. Often, the team has to provide emergency care to victims, which can lead to changes in the location. Let's look at the following example: a man is shot when he is sitting on the couch, being found lying on it. EMS evaluates the victim and verifies that the victim is in cardiac arrest. Then, move it to the floor to begin resuscitation. In this process of moving the victim to the floor, one of the members of the EMS, with his foot, drags a pile of papers on the floor. The victim is treated and transported without the police being informed of the position in which he was initially found. Police at the scene see blood on the couch, blood on the floor, and papers scattered on the floor, believing that a fight has occurred, resulting in two injured victims. Communicating the initial observations to the police and saying what was done on the scene will avoid confusion and false assumptions. Other important items to mention to the police: spontaneous statements by an offender or victim on the scene; suspicious things that have been viewed or heard; the conditions present when the team arrived; the extent of the victim's injuries, where the team will transport the victim; and other specific items to the location.

Here are some possible scenarios to occur:

1. The EMS arrives at the scene and finds an unconscious victim in a dark apartment. EMS turns on the light and finds a homicide victim. When did the crime occur? It probably occurred during the day, but the team, by turning on the light, changed the scene.
2. The team arrived at the scene and observed an unconscious victim lying on the floor near the door. Enter and start emergency care. When observing the victim, they realize that the victim suffered a head trauma due to assault. When the team is asked whether the door was open or closed, they cannot remember the exact answer.
3. The team arrives at the scene and a radio is playing loudly. The team turns off the radio to start resuscitation maneuvers, not informing the police that they had turned off the radio. The suspect later comes to confess that he heard the radio on and that he took the time to rob the house and only then killed the elderly man.

Communicating initial impressions to the police and reporting what has been done on the scene will prevent confusion and false ideas.

Conduct on the scene

For proper conduct on the scene, we must keep in mind some important rules. Thus do not dispose of disposable materials used during the intervention or material that is related to the victim, even if the articles are soiled with fluids. You must not move or touch anything or allow them to do so, except to provide medical assistance to the victim. After verifying that the victim has died, the team should try not to alter the crime scene and control entry to the scene, until the police arrive. If the victim is already found dead, for example, in the bedroom of a house, the evidences are not limited to just the bedroom. For example, the attacker may have washed his hands in the kitchen or in the bathroom, he may have gone to the bathroom to look for medicines, leaving shoe prints throughout the house. The attacker may have tried or even stolen objects in the house. If someone changes the location, they must inform the police (who changed the location, what changed it, and why they changed it). Do not make assumptions about victims or suspects and do not be inconvenient in comments [49].

What you should not do on the scene:

1. cut clothes through bullet holes, or cuts caused by a bladed weapon;
2. shake or turn clothes inside out;
3. leave medical supplies or gloves in scene;
4. trust in memory;
5. change the position of the vestiges unless absolutely necessary;
6. step on blood stains or drips;
7. touch weapons or ammunition.

Street

The information received by the 911 Call Center is important to ensure that the medical team is prepared to approach the scene properly. The 911 Call Center must therefore provide the following information to the medical team: pertinent information on weather conditions, adverse traffic conditions (roadblocks, roadblocks passages), faster and safer route, existence of associated risks (electricity pole fall, gas leaks, dangerous animals, fires, landslides), need for helicopter support. The first pieces of information (location and type of call) help to determine if there is a need for specialized help or extra equipment. The EMS usually has a desire to enter the scene and immediately start providing emergency care that can make you forget to protect the scene.

Reflective clothing should always be worn and ensure that there is a quick and safe exit location. When approaching a vehicle, it is recommended to approach with only one person. A colleague must remain in the ambulance, and this element has the possibility of obtaining good visibility, which makes it possible to record all suspicious actions of the vehicle's occupants. At night, the vehicle's lights should illuminate the interior of the vehicle and the surrounding area. Before approaching the vehicle, the possibility of using the sounder of the siren for identification and communication must be considered, thus allowing a response from the vehicle occupants [20].

Picture 14 — Sideways approach puts EMS at risk.

Picture 15 — Forward approach reduces risk but still puts EMS at risk.

Picture 16 — Correct approach that allows you to observe any suspicious movement inside the vehicle.

Picture 17 — A victim in a suspicious position.

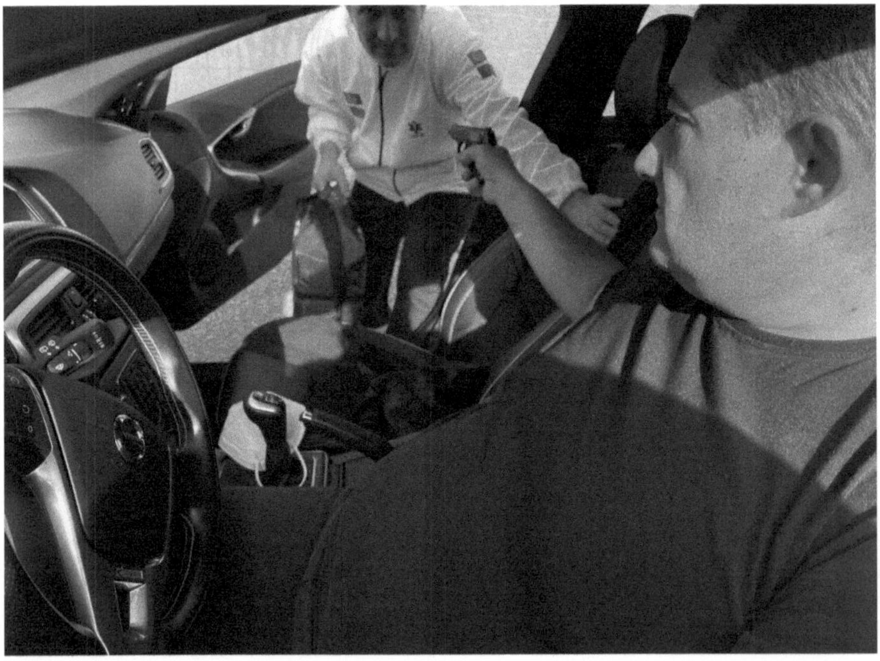

Picture 18 — Risks of the lateral approach. Armed victim at high risk of EMS.

The person approaching the vehicle must do so on the opposite side of the driver. In this way, you protect yourself from the traffic that may exist and approach the opposite side of the police [21]. Another precautionary measure is not to walk between the ambulance and the vehicle to avoid any injury if the vehicle recedes. Placing the vehicle in a queue can protect medical personnel in situations of gunfire. The EMS must be aware of any suspicious movements that occur inside the vehicle, especially in the back seat. The element that addresses the vehicle must observe the seats of the vehicle well, paying special attention, for example, to the existence of weapons and in the case of suspected risk, it must immediately leave the scene. If the passenger adjusts the rear or side mirror of the car while the medical team member approaches the vehicle, this is a danger sign. In places suspected of violence, the EMS must be attentive to everything around them. For example, graffiti walls may indicate a warning sign for violence (walls with words in reverse: LIVED, SANATAS, HTAED, LLIK) [21].

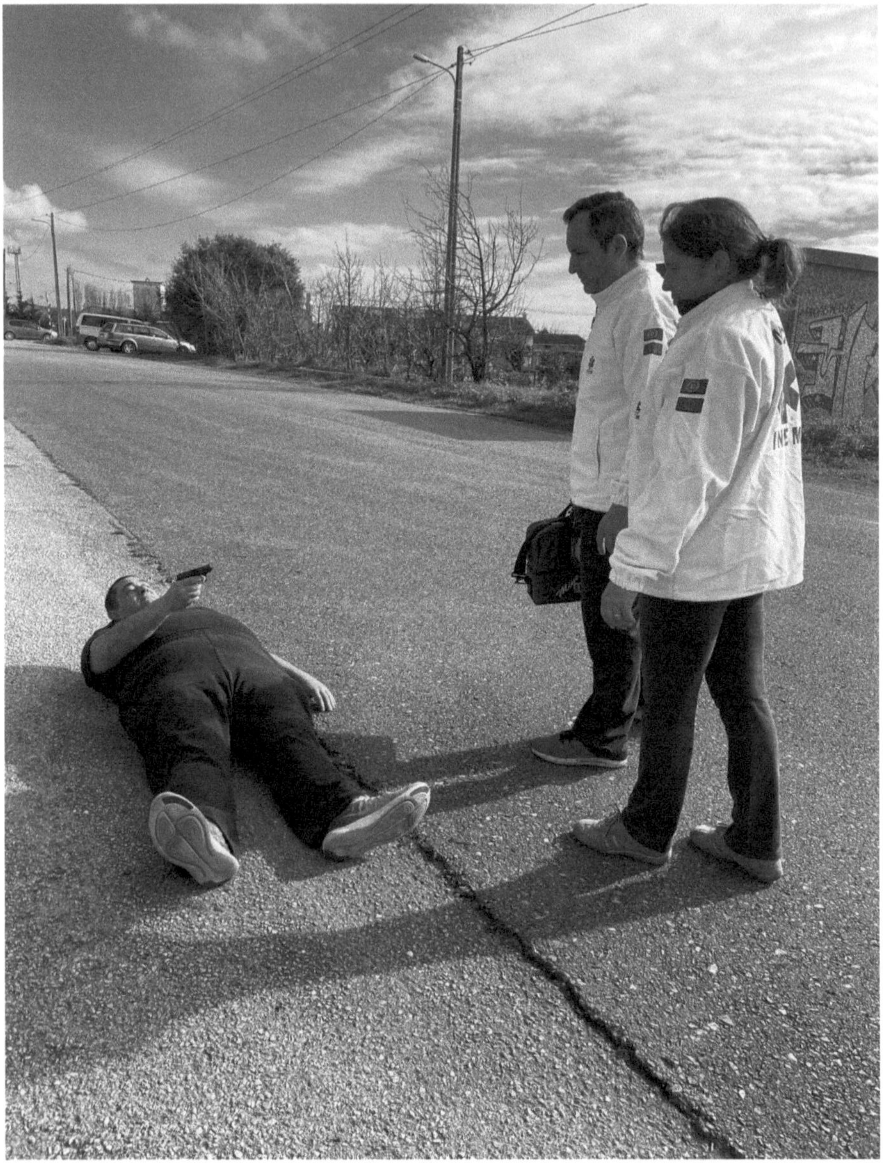

Picture 19 — Wrong approach to an armed victim. The EMS team is totally exposed to danger.

Picture 20 — Proper approach the victim will have to move backwards in case of assault and the EMS team can run away.

CHAPTER 10

Intervention in the preservation and collection of evidences

To systematize the intervention of emergency medical services (EMS), I will present the procedure in different situations. After a first approach to the body, to verify the death, one must examine the clothes and be careful with the fluids that may exist around the body.

External mechanical agents

Firearms injuries

Basically when a firearm is discharged, the following dynamics occur: fire or flame is emitted from the barrel. Smoke follows this flame, bullet emerges from the barrel, and additional smoke and grains of both burned and unburned gunpowder follow the bullet out the barrel. As this material exits the barrel, it spreads out like a funnel, as the distance from the barrel increases the density of the pattern decreases.

The flame does not go very far, the smoke goes a little further the powder grains travel different distances, and the bullet travels the greatest distance. The bullet perforates the skin and bores through, and the bullet entrance hole will be smaller than the actual projectile. There will be a blackening effect around the wound's edges caused by the discharge of lubricants, smoke particles, and grime from the barrel of the weapon.

When approaching the victim, it is normal for the wound to be exposed, for the treatment and the location of the bleeding. To assess the wound, it is necessary to remove the clothing, which often has holes that were caused by the bullet penetrating, or because there was a fight between the aggressor and the victim. These holes must be preserved for the criminal study; so, the clothes must be cut by the seams. The clothes may contain powder residues, emitted by the gases of the powder burning. EMS must describe the characteristics of the injuries, identify the entrance and exit of orifices (if any), describe their location (including

EMS in Crime Scene. DOI: https://doi.org/10.1016/B978-0-12-824420-3.00011-3

size), the presence or absence of bruise rings, and the presence of soot. EMS should avoid cleaning the wound as well as the victim's hands, which should be protected with paper bags (close with adhesive) [46].

Veins on the back of the hand should be avoided, preferably using central locations. In victims of gunshot wounds, care should be taken to bullets that are lost in their clothing, or their wrappers, which may be scattered. Bullets, ideally, should be left on scene. In cases involving the use of shotgun rifles, the team should try to recover the plastic bush (without causing significant changes to its shape), since it is an important element in determining the firing distance. Whenever possible, it is also important to indicate the location of the body from which the projectiles are taken and to reference them individually in the body diagram and in the notes.

Handling firearms at crime scene

When EMS arrive on a crime scene and find an unconscious victim with a firearm present, do not touch the firearm if you do not have to. Quickly move the patient away from the firearm. If you are assessing an armed patient who is conscious or may regain consciosness, do not hesitate to retreat from the scene and notify the police. If suggestions fail and you must move a firearm, do so with two considerations: safety and evidence preservation. Safety comes first. Never point the muzzle at anyone, including yourself. Never stick a pen or pencil into the barrel to move the firearm. Never touch the area around the trigger. Firing a gun when the hammer is cocked may take less than a pound of pressure.

With evidence preservation in mind, handle the gun by the top of the grip, near the frame with the muzzle pointed in a safe direction. Move the gun to a safe location, away from the patient and others, and place in a resting position with the muzzle pointed in a safe position. Again handle firearms only when absolutely necessary.

When examining the location, EMS, in cases of death by firearm, must record the following data:

- time when the victim was found;
- time when it was last seen;
- who found the victim;
- whether or not the weapon exists with the victim;
- characteristic of the weapon and its location;

- type of weapon;
- caliber and type of ammunition (if known);
- existence of projectiles fired at the location (number and location);
- existence of envelopes on scene;
- existence of marks of passage or impact of projectiles;
- objects on the periphery of the body; and
- description of the wounds and their location.

It is interesting to investigate whether the victim was displaced and, if so, in which direction he was displaced, the number of existing injuries and their anatomical location, and the existence or not of defensive injuries. The identified injuries must be documented in a body diagram. It is also important to check for the existence of projectiles trapped in clothing, which may fall with the mobilization of the body, or under the body, as well as any stains and fluids that may be in place and/or in the body.

Gunshot residue

In crimes involving gunshot wounds, it is often helpful to determine the distance from which the weapon was fired. Finding the proximity of the parties involved can often lend credibility to the victim's or suspect's claims of self-defense by distance determinantion using gunshot residue (GSR) patterns, and the absence of which would indicate that firing distance may not have been close range and therefore not likely self-defense.

The size and density of the power tatto pattern on the body around the wound of entrance can be used to determine the range at which the weapon was discharged by the replication of this pattern on test material (DiMaio).

GSR investigation focuses on the victim's body and clothing or other objects in the vicinity of the weapon fired. For the detection of residues in the hands, they must be protected with paper bags, for later performance of the paraffin test to detect the presence or absence of powder nitrates (procedure performed by criminal investigation).

The following vestiges must be preserved and collected:

- Weapon
- Cartridges

- Fired projectile
- Casing
- Collection and placement of clothes in paper bags
- Protection from injuries with sterile dressing, but without disinfection with betadine.

Differential diagnosis of medicolegal etiology

Deaths resulting from the use of firearms (homicide or suicide)	
Homicide	**Suicide**
Absence of evidences of gunpowder in the victim's hands	Hand(s) impregnated with gunpowder
Presence or absence of evidences on the victim's clothing and/or body	Presence of evidences
Entrance holes with any configuration	As a rule, irregular or starry edges
"Edges," which translate shooting at any distance	The edge usually translates into contact firing or very short distance (less than 15 cm)
Injuries can be found in any region of the body (vital or nonvital)	Lesions in vital regions (skull and cardiac region)
It may have several impacts	In general, only one impact

Bloodstain patterns

Bloodstain pattern analysis is done at violent crime scenes to help the investigator analyze the crime scene. Bloodstain pattern can provide many details:

- location and orientation of persons and/or objects at the time the blood was shed;
- minimum number of violent events (strikes, shots, etc.);
- area of origin for the trauma in three dimensions;
- type or category of weapon used;
- amount of force used to cause bloodshed;
- may help determine if the suspect was also injured;
- may help to confirm or refute a witness, suspect or victim statement.

Bloodstains patterns should be observed during the investigator's initial walkthrough. The blood will need time to dry in order for the stains to be properly analyzed. Every bloodstain pattern should be photographed and sampled for DNA. When analyzing bloodstain patterns, first divide the stains into three basic categories: active, passive, or transfer.

Analyzing bloodstain pattern

Impact spatter is the only pattern we analyze for the area of origin to determine where the victim was and when the event occurred. First, we must look the area of convergence and the area where the radiating pattern comes close together. This gives us one dimension. Then, we must find the angle of impact and string the stain or use lasers.

Bloodstain pattern documentation is like documenting any other item of evidence. Document must be taken care properly so that an analysis can be made. Swab the stain with moistened distilled water, and let it air dry before packaging. Record each droplet swabbed by pattern and location within pattern. Every pattern should be photographed all bloodstains patterns as a unit from all angles.

Stab injuries

An incision or cut-type wound is caused by a sharp instrument or weapon and is generally longer than it is deep. The cut or incised wound is deepest where the weapon was first applied to the skin. If the cutting is done parallel to the lines of cleavage, the edges of the wound will remain together. If the cutting is across the lines of cleavage, the wound will be gaping or open.

Incised wounds straight razor, the wounds are longer than deep and will bleed profusely. These types of injuries cut across the lines of cleavage and usually result in permanent scarring for victims who survive the assault.

Lines of cleavage or Langers lines—the cutting injury will appear slit-like when cut parallel to the lines of Langer. The cutting injury will have a gapping effect when perpendicular to the lines of Langer.

These injuries have little information about the object that was used. The team must observe the type of injury present and diagnose the presence or absence of defense wounds or hesitation wounds. Defensive wounds result from the defensive position taken by the victim, commonly located on the forearms and hands. If the wounds are located in the anterior parts, they are called "active defense" (they are located, above all, in the digital folds and palm), usually indicating that the victim fought. If they appear in the posterior parts (they are mainly located on the back of the hand and the external face of the forearm), they are "passive defense," indicating that the victim protected himself. Defense wounds give the indication that at least at the beginning of the attack, the victim was conscious, and that she was not caught off guard, having defended himself. On the other hand, the hesitation wounds are small in size, commonly located next to the most serious and profound injuries, which determined death, indicating in most cases that it is a suicidal act. The execution of these injuries is due to attitudes of experimenting with the blade of the weapon, hesitation, and fear of pain, being generally small superficial blows (1–2 cm) [15].

The nature of the injuries may offer investigators important clues concerning the death, for example, unusual number of wounds present suggesting an "over-kill" may indicate the perpetrator was acting in a rage at the time of the incident which may tend to suggest the perpetrator and victim knew one another as the assailant appears to have wanted to destroy not just kill the victim. Multiple stab wounds should red flag the investigator to the possibility of a sexual motive of the case.

The depth of the wound should be not used to gage the length of the knife. The knife may not have been inserted to its full extent, or the elasticity of the tissue involved may have allowed the knife blade to have traveled much further into the tissue due to the thrusting pressure associated with the insertion.

A contusion around a stab wound may be caused by the hilt of the weapon if sufficient force was used to thrust that weapon into the body. This contusion should be examined closely as a particular pattern may be present to align with the hilt of a particular weapon.

It is also interesting to investigate whether the victim has been displaced, whether there are signs of entrainment by the victim, the number of injuries and their anatomical location, and the presence or absence of self-inflicted injuries, hesitation injuries, and defense injuries, as well as other injuries.

Close physical contact had to have occurred between the victim and the assailant for the victim to have sustained sharp force injuries. The possibility for recovering meaningful trace evidence such as hair and fibers may be excellent. Examine the hands and fingernails of the body prior to bagging (paper) the hands and transporting the body to the morgue. You should also protect the victim's hands with paper bags and preserve any evidences that may be related to the case.

The weapon and possible toxics that may have been used must be preserved and collected. Wounds should be measured and documented on a body diagram. The edges must first be bonded with adhesive, for subsequent measurement of the wounds.

Clothing becomes critically important not only because of the possibility of trace evidence which may be present, but also the character and dimension of the offending weapon may be more discernible through examination of the wound especially in those cases involving a delayed fatal death.

Blood letting involving the decedent usually allows for the reconstruction of a preserved scene. Always X-ray the body who has been stabbed and/or cut. The possibility exists that the knife tip has broken off when striking bone and may still remain in the body.

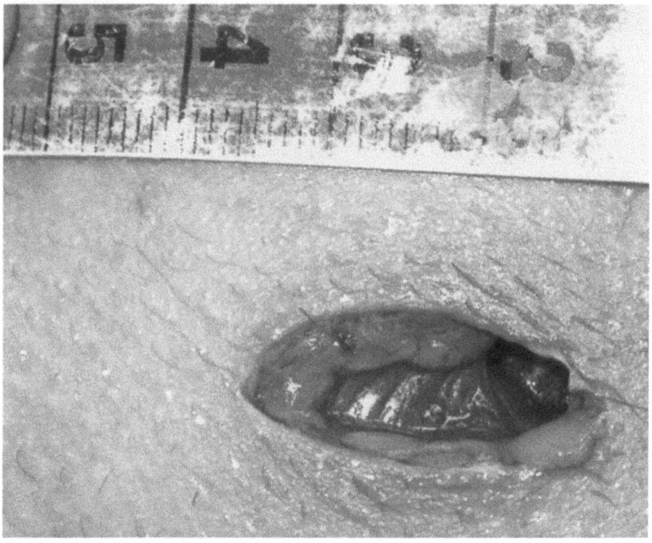

Picture 1 — Inaccurate measurement.

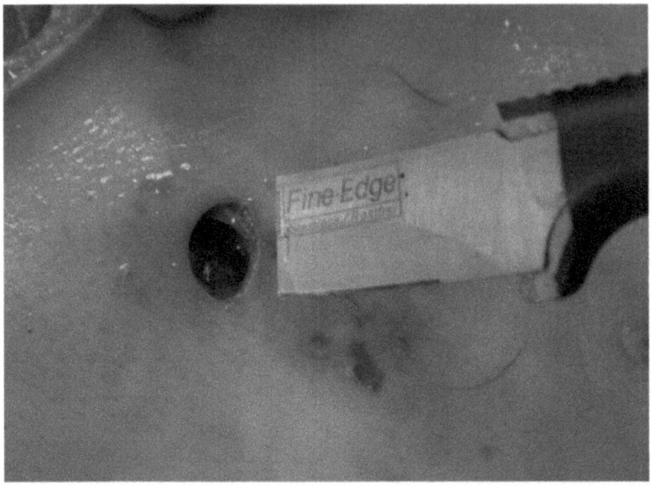

Picture 2 — Wound with widened edges without approximation of the edges, incompatible with the knife that appears in the image.

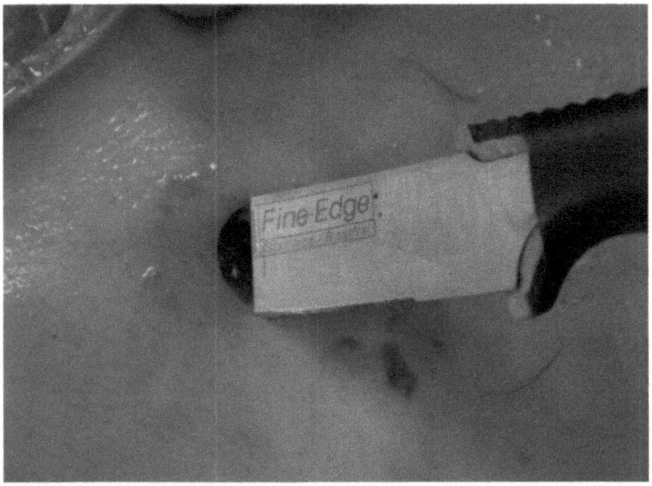

Picture 3 — By bringing the knife closer it is possible to see that it was the object that caused the wound.

When examining the scene, EMS, in cases of death by a stab, must record the following data:

- time when the victim was found;
- time when it was last seen;

- who found the victim;
- whether or not the weapon exists with the victim;
- characteristic of the weapon and its location;
- objects on the periphery of the body;
- description of the wounds and their location;
- describe exact position of the body;
- describe clothing worn by decedent;
- if present, describe exact position of knife or sharp-bladed instrument found in scene;
- describe the areas of apparent injury to the decedent;
- describe defense marks in body.

Blunt trauma

Blunt force injuries are usually evident by outward signs such as lacerations and bruising. However, lack of external injuries does not mean that blunt force was not applied. In many cases, internal damage to organs occurs without any external signs of violence. The abdominal organs are vulnerable to a variety of injuries because of the lax and compressible abdominal walls. Blunt injuries result from the application of force to the body over a large or small surface area resulting in damage to the tissues.

There are essentially four types of blunt trauma: abrasions, lacerations, bruises, and fractures. The determination of the type of trauma can be done by analyzing the injuries, as well as the circumstances that caused the injury.

Abrasions normally a superficial injury to the skin but may be associated with a more severe injury to the internal organs. In abrasions, the vestiges help the investigation, in determining the direction of the forces applied to the victim. Abrasions may become important because at the site of the injury, a patterned abrasion may be visualized. This patterned abrasion may be representative of the tool used to inflict the injury. Particles can be transferred from the object or surface to the wound. Often, wound dressings are performed at the accident scene; so, the medical teams in the hospital, when reworking the dressing, must keep the compresses previously placed on the wound, as they may contain important evidences. The clothing must be observed, as it may contain remnants of important material (earth, tar, stones, herbs, etc.). Ideally, healthcare professionals should describe the appearance of the wound and collect any evidences, before cleaning, disinfecting, debriding, or suturing the wound. Abrasions can provide important information, such as the direction of body movement and the distance covered.

Lacerations are generally poorly classified and are characterized by the presence of irregular edges, joined tissues, margins with edema, and localized contusion. Occur when the blunt force applied to the soft tissue stretches the skin past the point of elasticity resulting in the tearing of the issue. Lacerations of the scalp often resemble incised wounds. However, lacerations caused from blunt force can be distinguished from the incised injuries caused by sharp instruments by close examination of the wound. The direction of the force causing the laceration may also be determined through the examination of the wound.

Bruise is caused by breakage of small blood vessels with the blood moving into surrounding tissue. For their part, bruises that have different color patterns suggest that the injuries occurred at different times. For medical teams, the pattern of the injury can help to identify the object that caused them. Bruises require an exhaustive description; so, photo documentation in these cases is paramount. They may be associated with interpersonal violence, and their location may indicate whether the history provided is compatible with the injury or not.

Fracturing of the bone may occur as a result of the blunt force applied to the area. Blood vessels and nerves may be injured in areas associated with the facture. Bony fragments produced during the fracturing process may also produce contusions and lacerations. In fractures, it is important to assess the injury mechanism. Rotational injuries generally have spiral fractures and are often associated with child abuse.

Deaths from a blunt injury can be due to suicide, accident, or homicide.

The extent of blunt force injury is dependent on four factors:

- The amount of force applied.
- The length of time of the application of the force.
- The size of the area over which the force is applied.
- The elasticity of the organ receiving the force.

In homicide and death investigation, we look for impact injuries to the head which were caused by an object striking the head or the head striking an object. Homicidal deaths are characterized by localized violence and the use of some weapon. It may involve one blow or multiples blows. Suicidal deaths from blunt injury are most often seen in persons who have jumped from high places or thrown themselves into the path of a moving vehicle. Accidental deaths due to blunt force are most often due to a fall with injuries inflicted to the head and neck.

When examining the scene, EMS, in cases of death by blunt force, must record the following data:

- exact time of incident;
- exact time when body was found;
- describe place where body was found;
- describe exact position of the body;
- describe clothing worn by decedent;
- describe any other (possible) weapon and describe its location;
- describe any other item of potential evidence including blood spatter, overturned furniture, ransacked drawers, and suicide note;
- describe the areas of apparent injury to the body (inspect hands and arms for defense marks).

Motor vehicle accident (MVA) accidents

In these cases, it is important to know the position of the occupants when the accident occurred. Shattered glass will cause injuries to the face of victims in the front seats [7]. In contrast, the vehicle's side windows are made of tempered glass, which breaks into angled pieces, so they can cause angular injuries to the victim (on the side where the glass is). The glass shards must be collected and placed in solid packaging. Clothing should be preserved as it may contain evidences of contact with the car, the road surface, and other objects. The suit may also contain blood leftovers, which can give investigators an indication of the direction of force and injury. Ideally, before starting any activity, photograph the vehicle. In the event that this situation is impracticable, a description should be made as detailed as possible, with the description of the state of the vehicles, location or apparent position of the occupants, visible injuries, and probable trauma kinematics.

Determination of who was driving vehicle:

- No other occupant of vehicle.
- Wedged into drivers seat by instantaneous collapsing of cabin.

- Found in drivers seat with seat belt clasped.
- Injuries and blood letting of decedent is consistent with damage and blood spatter observed at the scene and in the vehicle.
- Trace evidence (hair, fibers, blood) from a particular area of the vehicle is consistent with the decedent being the operator of the vehicle.
- Brake or accelerator pedal impression on the sole of the shoe of the suspect operator of the vehicle.

Is essential some photographs: overview of an area, point of impact at scene, and photograph decedents vehicle and all other vehicles involved including exterior, tires of vehicle, and vehicle damage. Photograph the decedent.

EMS should describe condition of roadway, describe weather conditions, describe area and vehicles involved, describe impact site, and describe collision and driver behavior (windows upon vehicle, radio playing, air conditioner, or heater in the on position).

In cases where the vehicle or vehicles have suffered a fire, with the presence of occupant or occupants, having become carbonized, it is essential for the medicolegal investigation to collect material for identification and to determine the rate of carboxyhemoglobin [7]. It is also important to make a differential diagnosis between intravital injuries and injuries caused by fire, as well as researching the cause of death, which may indicate an attempt to conceal homicide or an accident.

The vehicles on fire need some care by the medical teams. Sometimes, the reading of evidences in fire scenarios is hindered by several factors: the damage caused by the fire itself, the existence of deceptive signs caused by different thermal loads in several locations that originate secondary foci more intense than the first ones [50]. There may also be a drop of material on the ground, and the combat and aftermath operations carried out by the firefighters themselves may alter the evidences. The team should always try to record the original and relative position of the displaced objects, as well as the damage that was caused by the combat operations and aftermath of the fire. In a fire situation in different contiguous areas, it is necessary to avoid, whenever possible, the transfer of materials and objects between these areas (choose a neutral area to place elements of furniture, carbonized, or partially carbonized clothing) [15]. It is also important to always record the state of the vehicle's doors and windows upon the arrival of the team, and whenever glass doors or parties are forced as a result of combat and aftermath operations, register this situation, and report it to the police authority. As far as possible, one should avoid moving materials and accessories from the vehicle and call the attention of firefighters to the use of high-pressure hoses, as these spread the materials a lot and destroy any evidences that may exist.

EMS must document the presence of odor from alcoholic beverages, the results of blood glucose measurements, and changes in the behavior of the victims, such as aggression, drowsiness, or slurred speech.

Run over

There are four different types of actions which may occur as a result of a vehicle striking a pedestrian. The classical impact involves the striking of an individual by a motor vehicle causing that person to be thrown onto the hood of a car. The primary impact of the vehicle involves the bumper bar striking the legs of the pedestrian usually resulting in the fracture of the tibia. The primary impact point is the best indicator of the pedestrian's position at the time of the impact.

An important measurement involves the distance from the ground (measured as the heel of the pedestrian's foot) and the point of the leg where the injury exists. This will roughly correspond with the height of the bumper at the time of impact.

Pedestrian versus a high vehicle (pick-up trucks and larger vehicles): The primary impact site is often higher than what is seen in a victim struck by an automobile. Patterned abrasions from the grill headlight and insignias (badges) of the involved vehicle may be present as patterned abrasions on the decedent.

Vehicle versus child: Because of their lower center of gravity, children will tend to be pulled under the vehicle rather than being knocked over the hood. Children are often hit by slower moving, backing-up vehicles. The bumper strikes the knee of the child causing the child's leg to become locked under the vehicle. Unable to free his/her leg, the child is pulled under and run over by the vehicle. The primary impact point will involve the knee or thigh (femur) of the victim.

Atypical actions involving vehicles versus pedestrians. No primary impact site is found on the calf of the decedent. Other injuries observed tend to indicate the victim may have been in an unusual position when struck by the vehicle.

In these cases, the contribution of the EMS is part of the preinvestigation phase. Teams must follow the following procedures:

- take a picture and set the scene;
- reference the positions of the point of impact (if there are vestiges), the location of the body, and the location of other vestiges;
- collect all evidences: plastic pieces, victim's clothing, and optical glasses (the identification of tiny glass particles is important to determine whether or not a suspect was present at the crime scene). The larger fragments are equally significant for the forensic scientist, in cases such as car accidents or running over with escape. Parts of the broken headlight can lead to the identification of the type and brand of the car from which they come.

Is very important to collect clothing of the decedent, separately bag each piece of clothing? Collect debris found on decedent's remains and also collect sheet used in transporting the body.

In fact, nowadays when there is so much talk about motor vehicle accidents, we must not forget the importance of lamps as evidence. In fact, an electric lamp can break accidentally or during a criminal action and break down (melt), while it is on or off. According to one of these situations or the combination of any of them, in the reading of the state of its filament, or filaments (in the case of road optics of motor vehicles), precious information can be collected, with relevant probative value in the investigation of a crime. [20] Thus these evidences must be collected, transported, and even previously examined at the accident scene. Given the delicacy of this evidences, it must be carefully picked and packed.

Although the expert examination falls primarily on the filament, it is advisable to collect all the elements of the lamp associated with it (glass, socket, etc.). In the case of sealed optics (integrated lighting systems where the entire headlight of the vehicle is a lamp), this set is carefully disassembled, on which the expert examination will be carried out.

The examination of filament lamps carried out by the scientific police leads us, in summary, to the following findings:

- The filament was new, used a lot or even very thin.
- The filament was whole, broken, or disconnected from its support.

- The filament was deformed or not.
- The filament was broken, with an abrupt fracture, or with rounded ends, terminated with fusion beads.
- The filament is oxidized, black, or iridescent, or covered with a yellow layer of tungsten oxide (W03), which can be blue.
- There is a complete absence of filament.

Before proceeding to the collection of lamps or optics, it should be noted which vehicle switches are connected, without, however, activating them, a fact that could lead to the destruction of the evidences. All fragments of lamp or sealed optics must be placed in a strong, clean and transparent plastic bag. The packaging must be inserted in a strong cardboard or wooden box and later handed over to the police[1].

Questions that the criminal investigation must answer:

- Was the accident the immediate cause of the victim's death? If not, what other factors contributed to the death?
- Are there serious illnesses on the victim from the autopsy? If so, did these illnesses contribute to the accident? If so, would a normal person have reacted differently to the accident?
- At the time of the accident, was the victim in full possession of his mental and physical faculties?
- What is the nature, shape, location, and extent of the victim's injuries?
- Was the vehicle colliding with the victim from the front or from the side?
- After the crash was projected or knocked over?
- Was the victim subsequently run over or pushed by the vehicle?
- Did the victim die immediately or did she undergo hospital treatment?
- Can the possibility of suicide or murder by a third party be admitted?

[1] Collection of lamps—Follow the traces of a concise report of the harvesting operations and the circumstances of the accident, including the exact time and detailed photograph of the crash zone. In the case of serious accidents, in which the analysis of the lighting system depends on the attribution of responsibilities, it is also advisable to remove all lamps from the affected area, even if they have not been affected by the crash, as they work as an indicator of the general state of the lighting system. before the accident and provide information on the impact of the crash by observing the deformation of the filament of the lamps in the absence of fracture of the glass bulb. Sometimes, the researcher is asked the question of in what space a vehicle can stop due to the braking system (foot brake). However, in ideal conditions of operation of the brake system (horizontal, dry) and condition of the tires, stopping is a natural function of your speed. Thus the formula: $M = V^2/100$ leads to the distance at which the vehicle can be immobilized. In the formula, "M" represents distance in meters and "V" represents speed. For example, if the vehicle runs at 30 km/h, the application of the formula is: $M = 30$ squared, over 100, so $M = 9$ m.

Death on the street

It constitutes a major challenge for EMS, since deaths that occur on the street can lead to many people involved at the scene of death. People can invade the scene and remove elements that may be important for the investigation. The area open to the public must be immediately isolated. As soon as the death is confirmed, the scene must be immediately sealed with bands and the police must be immediately activated.

Asphyxia

One area of prehospital that has an important impact on criminal investigation is the generic category of asphyxia. Without external signs of trauma, asphyxia can be difficult to identify at autopsy, so it is very important to document all the information about the accident or crime scene, to assist medicolegal investigation. Asphyxia is a condition in which the body becomes deprived of oxygen. Asphyxia normally occurs rapidly involving only a matter of minutes.

There are several means of achieving an asphyxial condition including the following:

Hanging

Body weight provides the force on a suspending rope or ligature. Most hangings are suicidal. Accidental hangings are uncommon, and homicidal hangings are extremely rare.

In a case of hanging, the EMS team, when arriving at the scene, must follow the following essential rules:

- If there are clear criteria for death, do not remove the body and wait for the police to arrive.
- Never cut the knot in the rope, because its location and the technique with which it was performed may be important for criminal investigation.
- If there are probable signs of life, you should remove the victim quickly, protecting him from any traumatic injury to the cervical spine and/or possible fall.
- Try to know the suspension time.

- Examine the area where the ligature is attached. Note any notched areas indicating possible prior acts or attempts.
- Examine the ligature for any worn areas or napping. Is there any indication the rope was used to hoist the weight (homicide) or pulled down (suicide or accident)?
- Analyze the disposition of livors in the body (tendency present in the slope areas).
- Place paper bags in the victim's hands.
- Inspect the hands and arms for defense marks.
- It is important to investigate whether the victim has been displaced and whether there are any other injuries that have not resulted from hanging.

In these situations, the medical team must record the following data:

- place of suspension[2] (assess the victim's accessibility to the suspension point);
- time when the body was found;
- time when the victim was last seen;
- who discovered the body;
- type of suspension (complete or incomplete suspension);
- nature of the rope material;
- describe the knot(s);
- groove type;
- type of knot and location;
- objects on the periphery of the body;
- describe the areas of apparent injury to the decedent;
- existence or absence of a farewell note;
- clinical history (psychiatric history, suicide attempts);
- other relevant data, which may be related to the case;

[2] Suspension—We can divide the suspension into incomplete and complete: Incomplete when there is a part of the body that is in contact with a surface; complete when there is no part of the body in contact with a surface.

Groove type—In the choke, the groove is horizontal, low. The constricting means are soft and there may be crossing of the two tops in the middle depending on the position of the aggressor. In the groove in hard environments, the skin is not free, there are parchment marks and hyperemia on the edges. When hanging, the groove is almost always incomplete and may have an inverted V shape. The scorched and parched groove, after death, has a high and usually ascending location. There may also be false furrows, which can be divided into: natural (always frequent in infants and obese); artificial (reproduce the object that produces them); pathological (caused by dermatosis, intertrigo); and putrefaction: (above and below necklaces, collars, etc).

- presence of strange odors;
- presence of medication, alcohol, and drugs on scene.

The EMS must preserve and collect the noose, any farewell notes that may exist or other written documents, as well as toxics or drugs that may be near the body, and that may indicate that they have been ingested by the victim.

Strangulation

Manual strangulation involves pressure being applied to the neck by hands or forearms. 911 Call Center dispatchers who receive calls for incidents involving domestic violence should consider, when appropriate, asking the interlocutor if they have been strangled or "suffocated." As strangulation incidents can result in late medical complications or even death, "shippers should consider the specific circumstances of each incident and assess the need to call for emergency medical help." Circumstances that may indicate the need to call for emergency help include, but are not necessarily limited to:

- difficulty breathing
- loss of consciousness
- memory loss
- dizziness, nausea, headache or disorientation during or after the incident
- loss of vision or vision changes
- hearing loss or hearing changes
- voice changes or difficulty speaking
- cough or difficulty swallowing or feeling something in throat
- sore throat
- problems with balance or coordination
- pain or stiffness in the neck.

Ligature strangulation the mode of death is the constricting pressure is applied by some force other than body weight. Most deaths are by homicidal means. There are some suicides and accidental deaths associated with ligature strangulation.

In homicide cases the victims tend to be people less able to defend themselves from a more aggressive assailant. Bruising and linear abrasions may be present on the neck as the victim struggles in her/his efforts to dislodge the article.

In strangulation, medical teams must pay attention to the following aspects:

- taking photographs
- protection of hands with paper bags
- collection and storage of clothes
- toxic that may have been ingested
- do not remove rope from the neck
- observe possible signs of sexual assault.

The color of the face, the presence or absence of protrusion of the tongue, the existence or absence of an ecchymotic mask, and the presence or absence of nail stigmas, of defensive lesions, or signs of entrainment [51] should be investigated. Be cautious as to the possibility of innocent neck marking, which may appear on certain cases, being interpreted as ligature markings. The records, in this case, must include the following data:

- time when the body was found;
- time when you were last seen;
- who discovered the body;
- whether or not there is a loop around the body;
- nature of the loop material and type of groove;
- type of node and location;
- toxic substances that have been used, namely intravenously;
- existence or not of an equimotic mask;
- existence or not of nail stigmas;
- whether or not there are defense injuries.

Chocking

Requires an obstruction within the airway. Death is normally associated with accidental means and is normally influenced by intoxication, senility, and natural illnesses such as Parkinson's disease. Alcohol consumption is a common finding in these deaths.

In cases of choking, medical teams must make the following records:

- time when a corpse was found;
- time when it was last seen;
- who found it;
- existence or not of nail stigmas (distribuition and orientation in the neck);

- objects on the periphery of the body;
- everything that seems relevant;
- existence or not of an equimotic mask;
- whether or not there are defense injuries.

It is also important to protect the hands with paper bags and preserving any evidences that appear be related to the case is also important.

Smothering

In deaths due to smothering, asphyxia occurs by obstructing the respiratory openings by covering the nose and mouth of an individual or by the placement of the individual in a container devoid of a sufficient amount of oxygen.

Unless a gag or other item such as sand packed into the airway or a plastic bag is found over the head, autopsy findings will usually be incloncusive. Therefore in these types of cases, the circumstances of the death developed through careful investigation may be more important than the autopsy findings.

If a plastic bag is found over a decedent's head, it should be noted that it is not necessary for the bag to be completely sealed. The bag needs only to be placed in such as a way as to affect the normal exchange of gases.

Whenever a bag is encountered under these circumstances the bag should be immediately placed into a paint can and sealed for toxicological testing. Check all trash cans for discharged plastic bags.

Traumatic crush asphyxia

In this asphyxial type of death an external compressive force prevents the chest from engaging in normal respiratory movements. Most of the deaths associated with this method are accidental in manner. A few homicides have been reported. Death is normally influenced by intoxication, senility, and natural illnesses or disability. External examination of the body may show lines of pressure on the skin with forcible redistribution of blood noted. This will appear as an intense congestion of the head and neck and possibly the limbs depending on the position of the weight and the posture of the individual during the incident.

Postural asphyxia

Is a phenomenon occurring when a person's bodily position results in a partial or complete airway obstruction? It will usually involve the following:

- The decedent is discovered in a position not conducive to breathing. Normally this may involve a restrictive or confining position; however, it may also involve simple flexion of the head onto the chest a partial or complete airway obstruction or neck compression.
- Investigative information indicates the decendent inadvertently placed himself in this confining position without the deliberate action of another person.
- There is an absence of any other possible cause of death.

Drowning

Includes apparent drownings in pools, rivers, lakes, oceans, and any other body of water. Includes also near drowning deaths. Near drowning deaths are delayed fatal deaths where the subject survives a near drowning episode but later, succumbs to complications associated with the incident. Does not include scuba deaths. Drowning death is a death diagnosed by exclusion. There are no gross autopsy findings of significance that directly indicate the individual die as a result of drowning.

In drowning the objective of the investigation is the differential diagnosis of the cause of death, as well as the determination of its circumstances. EMS must respect the following rules:

- check if any witnesses witnessed the incident (if the victim asked for help);
- How long after the body was discovered and how long it was missing;
- description of water: depth, distance from sand, currents, the presence of stones or rocks, and probable temperature of the scene;
- description of clothing (had decedent removed coat, shoes, or valuables prior to entering the water);
- description of the body: visible wounds, appearance, and general condition;
- any evidence of alcohol.

The fact that a body is found underwater or shows signs of being immersed does not necessarily mean that the death was the result of submersion.

Sexual abuse

Most victims of sexual abuse are transported to the hospital by the police or by family members. It is necessary to approach the victim calmly and empathetically, as well as providing immediate privacy and avoiding public exposure of the victim. Victims become more collaborative with medicolegal procedures, which are part of assessing victims of abuse, if the first approach is supportive.

When approaching the victim, medical teams should know that they should only touch the areas of the body necessary for the stabilization and assessment of the victim, being very careful about exposure. They should avoid examining the perineal region, only in case of signs of bleeding. If the victim is at home and has changed clothes, you should request the clothes used during the abuse, preserve it, and placing it in paper bags in order to accompany the victim.

All elements that contact victims of abuse must understand the general principles of forensic science. Emergency teams that first approach victims of abuse should address injuries properly and treat them correctly. Severe trauma to victims of abuse is rare; so the victim's physical needs are limited. Screening for proper treatment should be based on the extent of injuries and the ease of resources for forensic analysis. Most victims should be taken to a hospital unit that is easy to provide forensic assessment of injuries, collection of evidences, and appropriate treatment of injuries [20].

The importance of clothing to medicolegal expertise should be explained to the victim. You should also document any information that the victim has voluntarily referred about the abuse and describe that it was the victim's voluntary statement with a description of their exact words. It is important to keep the sheet of the ambulance stretcher where the victim was lying, as it may contain evidences (fibers, hair, garbage, etc.), placing it in a sealed and identified paper bag [15].

In sexual abuse in general, the physical injuries that the woman may have are the following: lacerations, bruises, abrasions, and contusions. Sometimes injuries can be difficult to observe, as abusers often use sufficient force to obtain cooperation from the victim, and also because the phenomenon known as tonic immobility[3] of the victim can occur. Some methods used by these attackers may include snapping, grabbing, strangling, pulling hair, cutting, biting, and limb restraint. In the presence of injuries, the team must describe them objectively and in terms of anatomical location, from left to right, from the inside out. Approximate size, the presence of hemorrhage, deformity, and tissue color. The prehospital approach should focus your attention on areas of discomfort and pain and, if possible, not remove clothing.

Emergency care for these wounds should be limited to preserving life and function. The principle of forensic science is that any biological evidence can potentially contain DNA. The teams must not wash the wounds, especially the bite marks, as they may contain DNA, which can allow the identification of a genetic profile, through the aggressor's saliva. Ice application should be avoided as a way of reducing edema, as it is important not to affect the visualization of the wound for further photography.

Child abuse

EMS must perform a thorough examination of the child's body, paying special attention to the so-called hidden areas (soles, groins, armpits, and scalp). Physical abuse is the most commonly reported type of abuse and is manifested through bruises, burns, ligature marks, fractures, and disorders involving the central nervous system. Eye injuries, such as retinal hemorrhages, can be signs of abuse as well. The most common signs of abuse are the three B's: burns, breaks, and bruises.

It is imperative for the EMS professional to thoroughly assess and examine every child the same way every time so you do not miss any areas. A call with a higher index of suspicion is all the more reason to fully expose the patient.

Also observe the housing conditions and family environment. The team must speak separately with the caregivers, questioning the circumstances of the injury, and comparing the reported stories [52]. When teams are in the

[3] Tonic immobility—This is an autonomous response, which means that it is uncontrollable. It is not something that a victim decides to do. It is a mammalian response, and it is evolutionarily linked to protection and survival, because often the safest thing to do is protection and safety. At the behavioral level, it is marked by an increase in respiratory rate, by the closing of the eyes, but the most striking feature of tonic immobility is muscle paralysis. A victim in a state of tonic immobility cannot move his arms or legs.

scene, they can check the logic of the story. For example, if there is a child who has burns that the parents say was caused by the heater, it is imperative to observe the location and the respective heater, to check whether it is turned on or not. Always see the injury mechanism and compare injuries and circumstances with the location. Health professionals should photograph the child with and without clothes, observe the state of nutrition and general condition, and document all injuries found, body position, and family history [15].

When documenting a suspected nonaccidental trauma case remember that your job is not to assume, it is to be as descriptive as possible in presenting the facts. The information should be objective not subjective. Provider's must document important information about the scene and the patient's position. This is especially true when a patient is found in cardiac arrest. It is also vital to document what you see, hear, and smell, and what you are told about the incident.

Injuries associated with child abuse

Body area	Injury	Mechanism
Lip	Contusion	Direct blow
Frenulum	Laceration	Direct blow
Tongue	Laceration	Forced feeding
Ear	Hematoma	Direct blow
Nasal septum	Deviation/hematoma	Direct blow
Eye	Hematoma, Hyphema, and subconjuntival	Direct blow
Head and CNS	Subdural hematom	Direct blow. Shaking
Head and CNS	Cephalhematoma	Hair pulling
Thorax and abdomen	Hemothorax, Pneumothorax, and tears of mesentery	Direct blow
Ribs	Fracture	Direct blow
Legs/arms	Spiral fracture	Twisting of extremity
Legs/arms	Avulsion	Jerking of extremity
Palms of hand, soles of feet, or buttocks	Small circular burns	Cigarette burns
Buttocks, feet, and/or hands	Scalding with clear mark of demarcation	Immersion in hot water
Wrists, ankles, and mouth	Contusions and abrasions	May indicate previous use of bindings
Lower back	Contusions	Corporal punishment

(*Continued*)

(Continued)		
Body area	**Injury**	**Mechanism**
All areas	Oval abrasions with marked pattern	Bite mark
Hymen	Laceration	Possible recent sexual assault
vulva	Hematoma	Recent sexual assault
Fourchette	Laceration	Recent sexual assault
Anus	Laceration	Possible recent sexual assault

Child death

Four possibilities in dealing with the death of a child:

1. natural death with well-documented history;
2. sudden infant death syndrome;
3. accidental death of a child. Bed clothing (pillows, blankets, and sheets) by itself will not appreciably diminish oxygen intake of the infant and thereby cause the suffocation of the infant;
4. child may die as a result of child abuse. The investigation should be directed toward the identification of historical hints, social stresses, medical findings, and circumstantial risk factors which predisposed the dead child to lethal child abuse or neglect.

Documentation in this case

- When did injury occur? Who had access to the child?
- What was the time of death?
- Document medical history of the child
- Document family history
- Identify red flags
- Describe the condition of the interior of the home including cleanliness, lighting, and necessary facilities
- Describe any foul odors
- Any indication of heavy alcohol or drug abuse within the residence
- When was the child last seen alive?
- Describe the circumstances of the death as reported
- Describe the position of the body when found
- Describe clothing found on the decedent

Put bag in the hands of the decedent prior to transporting. If bite marks are present on the child, do not touch this area and notify the forensic odontologist.

Sudden infant death syndrome

EMS are the first to arrive at the scene, and in these special cases, three basic rules must always be kept in mind: give medical assistance if necessary, support the family, and observe and describe the scene. After verifying the death, the teams' attention should be on the description of the infant's external habit, on the scene where the infant was found, and on the conditions of the scene, with special attention to room temperature. Question parents separately about the event, to reduce the possibility of rehearsed stories. It is recommended to ask open-ended questions, as they provide better information.

According to Bledsor [53], the questions should include the following:

1. Can you tell me what happened?
2. Where was the baby?
3. Who found the baby? When?
4. What did you do when you found the baby?
5. Was the baby moved?
6. When was the baby last seen alive?
7. How was the baby today?
8. Has the baby been ill recently?

EMS should remember that SIDS[4] is a tragic and devastating event for the family; so their collaboration can be difficult. It is also one of the most stressful events that occurs in the prehospital. When the baby's death is determined, the parents and family become the victims. EMS must remain calm, objective, and professional. The emergency team plays a very important role in explaining to family members the medicolegal significance of the postmortem examination, and what steps will take place during the investigation of the case. The family should be asked about the child's health, sleeping conditions, and history of events before the child's death.

[4] SIDS—risk factors: Prone position or prone position during sleep, overheating, not breastfeeding and smoking. What should the pathologist do in case of SIDS? Do not pass complacency death certificates; systematically autopsy all cases of apparently healthy children who died suddenly and inexplicably; always follow the same autopsy protocol asking the Delegations of the National Institute of Forensic Medicine the respective complementary exams; carry out, before the autopsy, a detailed examination of the site and collect all information about the circumstances of death, taking into account the most frequent risk factors and etiologies; complete the SMSL survey in detail by interviewing parents or family members. When in doubt about the cause of death, you should seek, through the attending physician, to be aware of the clinical history or other means to arrive at your diagnosis, as rigorous as possible. You must not try at all costs to find a cause of death. When a cause of death is not diagnosed, you must write "Sudden Infant Death Syndrome" on the death certificate.

Communication with the family is imperative during this period, as its members are very vulnerable and in shock after death. Medical staff can be an excellent bridge between the family and support services.

Documentation

- Who was the last person to see the child alive? Date and time
- Who discovered the dead infant?
- What was the place of death
- Position of the infant when found dead
- Was resuscitation attempted?
- Any medical treatment
- Was the baby exposed to any illnesses recently?

Infanticide

Infanticide is the death of the newborn caused by the mother herself. Often, this death is associated with a state of mental disorder on the part of the mother, which may have different etiologies and etiopathogeneses. One of the challenges of forensic medicine is the demonstration that the baby had autonomous breathing, which has been the most used basis to prove the birth of the newborn with life, thus being able to distinguish between infanticide and abortion. Thus it becomes essential to classify the birth of the newborn with life as infanticide. In an autopsy room, the called Galen's hydrostatic docimacia[5] test (placing a lung fragment in a container with water). However, it is important to note that if there was a medical intervention with cardiorespiratory resuscitation, it may interfere with this test, since the lungs may have been inflated by mechanical

[5] Hydrostatic docimasia—Highly valuable, since it can be demonstrated with great reliability that the respiratory function was performed by the baby's lungs once the fetal-placental respiratory function has ceased. It is based on the physical phenomenon of density (taking into account that the density of water is 1). Changes in lung density due to breathing are studied, since the specific weight of the fetal lung is 1.5, whereas when breathed, the density decreases to 0.7, as it penetrates the air, its weight decreases and its volume increases. It consists of testing whether the lungs float or sink. In the first case, the baby breathed, and in the second case, he was born dead. The test consists of four times: FIRST TIME: The block formed by the lungs, heart, and thymus, dividing the trachea in its upper portion and in the esophagus and vessels at the level of the diaphragm, is placed in a container with water.

Positive: the block floats. Negative: it sinks. SECOND TIME: One lung is whole and the other is cut into small fragments, both being placed in the water. Positive: if everyone floats. Negative: if everyone sinks. THIRD TIME: Several pieces of lung are compressed firmly in the water, then they are cut by section and are observed. Positive: fine, homogeneous and abundant air bubbles are released, which foam on the surface. Negative: there are no bubbles. FOURTH TIME: The lung fragments that have floated and are violently compressed or crushed between the fingers against the container are taken, then placed in the container. Positive: they float. Negative: do not float.

or manual ventilation. Once again, it is extremely important for the medical team to document the resuscitation maneuvers that have been performed.

Domestic violence

The calls received by EMS for cases of domestic violence are always considered as potentially dangerous places. One of the strategies must involve the immediate activation of the police, in order to maintain security on the scene. When approaching the scene, the team should look around the place and see if there are lights on in the house, and if there are signs of struggle, shouting, crying and discussion. The safety of the team is a priority over medical assistance.

The EMS should make a checklist of questions:

- Should the team get closer?
- Are there any obvious dangers in approaching?
- Is there a previous history for other calls like this?
- What are the team's limitations?
- What help is available?
- When did the call occur (at night, during the day)?

The EMS must visually monitor the presence of weapons and determine who is in the residence and where they are. Once the people involved have been identified, they should be asked to leave. Residents should not be allowed to stay between the team and the exit, it is important to observe the body signals of all people present at the scene.

In addition to the dynamics of the location, it may be necessary to observe aggressive behavior before even approaching the victim to provide medical assistance. Avoid touching or crowding an already hostile person, as this can lead to more violent behavior. One should not be threatening, but stay lunch, take a balanced posture, and take nothing for granted. You must take control of the situation slowly. So you must introduce yourself, speaking directly to the victim, and explain what you are going to do. Open-ended questions are relevant, allowing them to speak. Do not show a critical posture. If possible, it is essential to separate the victim from the aggressor—a justification may be that you have to use equipment that is in the ambulance.

Evaluation of injuries

Accurate and thorough evaluation is the first step in establishing a relationship of trust with the victim of domestic violence. The assessment process is the first step in documenting injuries. The assessment also provides information about the resources and services available, while determining the lethality of the situation through sensitive questions.

The assessment of injuries in the presence of the partner puts the victim at risk. You can help the team if you maintain eye contact with the victim; however, this situation may be inappropriate for some individuals or cultures. Thus trust is a necessary component in the assessment. In an environment of privacy and security, you should allow the victim to describe his situation. The aggressors, with great conscience, reach areas of the body covered by clothes. For this reason, one should be wary of isolated bruises on the abdomen or a bruise on the face, especially if it is attributed, for example, to collisions with doors and/or cabinets.

Documentation

Well-documented cases are more likely to result in appropriate legal action against the offender. Therefore it is important to document inconsistencies between the victim's injuries and the history or description of the injury mechanism, providing descriptive details of the injuries. If, for example, a bruise on the face has the impression of a hand and fingers, this information should be noted, as well as the conditions of the residence, including broken furniture, holes in the walls or doors, clutter or broken glass. It is also important to identify weapons if present or used.

Security in the location of domestic violence

On the way to location:

1. Was the police sent? How far is it?
2. Were there comparable calls to this residence in the past?
3. Is the team prepared and equipped for this call? Preparation includes not only equipment, but also mental and emotional preparation.

Scene approach:

1. Approach with sirens and lights out. Stop the vehicle 200 m from the scene to gather additional tracks.
2. Are there items in the yard or garage that indicate that children may be present?

3. Is there any indication that firearms may be present in this residence?
4. If it is a night call, are the lights on in the house?
5. Is the vehicle parked for an escape route, if necessary?
6. What is the noise level in the residence? Are there screams or fighting sounds?

Entrance to residence:

1. Do not stand in front of an open door. When entering a room, turn on the lights. Leave the lights on in all rooms, if possible.
2. Are there any indications of alcohol or drug use in this residence?
3. Identify how many people are in the residence and where they are located. Never walk down a corridor with someone behind you.
4. If possible, do not work in kitchens or bedrooms: kitchens have several and one potential weapons, including knives, heavy pots, or glasses, for example. Rooms generally do not have an exit or escape route, and many people keep weapons hidden and loaded in this space. Finally, if the attacker has a jealous nature, the room can be seen as an intimate and therefore threatening place.
5. Do not assume that just because the attacker was arrested on the scene, the situation is under control. The victim or family members, even children, are known to attack the police as well as the emergency teams.
6. Determine the location and condition of the victim and separate the suspect and the attacker, if they are still in place. Interview the victim and any witnesses separately, especially if they are both injured.
7. Keep the exit path open at all times.

Burn

Most of the times, burn deaths present the accident as medicolegal. Accidental etiology can come from explosions, electrical burns, chemical burns, or fire. Associated with these accidents are often factors such as age, pathological history (epilepsy, stroke), ingestion of drugs that alter the state of consciousness, difficulties in locomotion, reaction time, alcohol and narcotic consumption, and negligence. Regarding the suicidal and homicidal medicolegal etiology, it is sometimes very difficult to distinguish, with the pattern of wounds playing an important role here. In cases where homicide occurs, most of the time we speak of passionate crimes. There is also the possibility of attempting to hide a body [15].

The role of EMS in these cases is based on the estimate of the burned area surface, the detailed description of the location and depth of the injuries, and the photographic record of the burn injuries and other traumatic injuries. Once again, the victim's clothing and assets are very important items for identifying the victim and reconstructing the events. The team should investigate the victim's pathological and therapeutic history, as well as possible psychiatric history, alcoholic habits, and drug use [15].

Collecting information from the family about the circumstances of the accident and others that may be important for the possible determination of the medicolegal etiology of the burn is crucial. If medical assistance has been provided to the victim, it is necessary to record what has been done and administered, especially invasive interventions such as escharotomies. Particular attention should be paid to clothing, with regard to damage caused by encrustation of metallic objects. At the same time, a careful examination must be carried out to determine which agent caused the burns.

In cases of death by electrocution, the preservation and collection of evidences consists more in the collection of information and documentation. As such, the following data should be recorded:

- time of occurrence;
- scene characteristics (soil/ground, type of material and professional equipment, sources of electricity and atmospheric conditions);
- information about the victim (profession, working hours, physiological conditions (fatigue, sweating);
- Description of the body's external habit.

It is important to examine clothing thoroughly, describing the type of clothing (conductive or insulating material), the condition of the clothing (dry, damp, or wet) and the relationship of the garments with the passage of the chain. Likewise, one must examine the body surface, discriminating against injuries resulting from the action of electricity and observing the existence of injuries resulting from falls, explosions, etc. Document if firefighters noticed odor of gasoline or other accelerant. The condition of the scene based upon the fire department's operations (body moved, debris removed, building collapse).

Investigation: was the fire intentional or accidental? Was the victim alive or dead before the fire?

Electrocution deaths

The death of a person as a result of electrocution occurs when that person becomes part of the electrical circuit. Electrocution can result from four electrical conditions:

1. Low-voltage alternating current
2. Low-voltage direct current
3. High voltage
4. Lightning.

First focus is distinguishing natural deaths from low-voltage electrocutions. Low-voltage electrocution deaths may not be discernible through autopsy. High-voltage deaths are fairly obvious. Although most electrocution deaths are accidental in nature, a minute amount may involve homicidal or suicidal actions.

Documentation

- Body position relative to the scene
- Electrical damage present
- Any injuries involving decedent
- Describe the location of the decedent
- Describe any electrical apparatus which may be present and possibly involved in the decedent's demise
- Describe clothing worn and note any damage areas
- Note any efforts of resuscitation.

Toxic external agents

Examining the scene is extremely important, as is collecting information. From the analysis of all the data collected, one can, in fact, reach the differential diagnosis: accident, suicide, or homicide.

Overdose/poisoning

When approaching a victim who is suspected of having overdosed, care should be taken to collect the suspected substance. Vials, tablets, and syringes should be stored and handled with care. Thus in order to preserve the content and possible fingerprints, teams should wear gloves or hemostatic forceps to remove the contents of the drugs in a paper envelope. When faced with a case involving suspected poisoning or overdose by injection, the coroner may have difficulty in determining which of the punctures are therapeutic and which ones were for puncture of the illicit substance. To assist in this determination, medical teams must mark with a circle (using a permanent marker) the places of therapeutic puncture, thus helping to distinguish between the two types of puncture. All evidences must be preserved (syringes with remains, and vomit must be aspirated into a sterile container and kept).

The examination of the scene, in cases of death from poisoning, requires the registration of the following data:

- time when the victim was found;
- time when it was last seen;
- who found the victim;
- product packaging that may have been used;
- signs of substance use intravenously;
- toxic that may have been used;
- clinical history;
- smells present on the scene;
- amount of gastric content;
- amount of substance(s) ingested.

The team must also investigate whether the victim has been displaced, the color of the face (congestion, pallor, vomiting, injuries caused by the action of caustic products), and the presence or absence of odor. It is important to describe the type of vomit, appearance, color, and odor and to collect it. Also record the existence of hemorrhage, seizures, electrocardiogram (ECG) changes, which the victim has presented before dying. In relation to the collection and preservation of evidences, all toxic substances that have been used, remains of the suspect product, the packaging of medications that are in place, as well as the coverslips must be collected. Syringes, needles and paraphernalia must be collected (in the case of drug addicts). If there are farewell notes or other documents, they must also be collected. All items must accompany the body to the morgue.

Ethanol

Alcohol assumes an importance in clinical forensic medicine because of its link with criminal activity. Traffic accidents, suicide, and rape are correlated with the concurrent use of alcohol. Child physical and sexual abuse, spouse abuse, and elder abuse are also associated with alcohol use.

Ethanol, also known as ethyl alcohol, drinking alcohol or grain alcohol. It is produced by the enzymatic action of yeast on carbohydrate in the absence of oxygen (fermentation). Absorption is by passive diffusion. Can happen in any part of the gastrointestinal tract. Mostly in stomach (20%) and upper small intestine (80%). Peak concentration is reached 30–60 minutes after ingestion.

Acute alcohol intoxication, or alcohol poisoning, can occur after the ingestion of a large amount of alcohol. Alcohol abuse differs from alcohol dependence, or alcoholism, in that it does not include loss of control over drinking or an extremely strong craving for alcohol. Abusers are not necessarily physically addicted to alcohol but develop problems as a result of their alcohol consumption and poor judgment, failure to understand the risks, or lack of concern about damage to themselves and others. Because they are not addicted, alcohol abusers remain in control of their behavior and can change their drinking patterns in response to explanations and warnings.

Investigation—Blood sample. Venopuncture in the crook of the elbow. Do not use any antiseptic that contains alcohol.

Carbon monoxide intoxication

In these cases, the objective is, first, to understand whether the medicolegal etiology is an accident or suicide and then to identify the probable source of carbon monoxide[6]. The performance protocol is as follows:

- description of the location;
- what is the likely source? For example, if a car is involved, check if the ignition is on, the fuel level, engine temperature, if the doors are

[6] Carbon monoxide—The pathophysiological mechanisms responsible for the systemic and neurological changes caused by CO are anemic hypoxia, arterial hypotension and, possibly, a direct neurotoxic mechanism still unknown. The neurological manifestations of CO poisoning are varied, ranging from confusion states to changes in the level of consciousness with the onset of coma, pyramidal and extrapyramidal symptoms and psychiatric syndromes. The neuropathological changes described in CO poisoning are necrotic lesions of the basal ganglia, ischemic or hemorrhagic brain injuries, cortical or subcortical, demyelination of the peripheral nerves and nerve roots, as well as degeneration of the posterior spinal cord.

closed, if there are suicide notes, describe the body's position, and if it is closed inside the car;
- photograph of the scene;
- description of the external body habit;
- difference of odors in the scene.

Sudden death

Sudden death is defined as a natural, unexpected fatal event, in an apparently healthy subject or one whose disease was not so severe enough as to predict such an abrupt outcome. In forensic sense, most of such deaths die in minutes or even seconds of the onset of symptoms. Its difficult to find the exact classification of sudden unexpected deaths, the problem comes from the definitions of both sudden and unexpected.

Examination at the scene of the death may present potential solutions to the problems of the death's classification: Any suggestion for "foul play"; eliminate suggestions of electrocution; evidence of planning for death (e.g., suicide notes); evidence of medication containers.

Special problems arise in certain cases and situations, because they require more investigation than usual, and because they have the most potential for serious error:

- No identification
- No cause of death
- Environmental exposure
- Decomposed body
- Skeletal remains
- Deaths in police custody and police shootings
- Mass disaster

Cardiovascular disease is the most common cause of sudden unexpected deaths in adults. Most of cardiovascular diseases related deaths are mainly due to coronary atherosclerosis.

Sudden unexpected death in Epilepsy is a term used when a person with epilepsy suddenly dies, in whom a postmortem examination fails to uncover a gross anatomical, toxicological or environmental cause of death. Death in an epileptic patient could be by asphyxia during a fit in bed when the face is pressed into the pillow. Also it may cause due to traumatic deaths because of fits occurring when patient in some vulnerable position and antiepileptic drug overdose.

Data collection (especially) on unidentified body

For data collection, it is essential to remove the body completely and analyze:

- Morpho-physiological structure and physiognomy (sex, race, stature, physique, probable age, features, color of eyes, hair, etc.);
- Congenital signs: particular signs/birth that assist identification;
- Dental formula: (teeth can provide information about the victim's identification, race, eating habits);
- Osteoanthropometric examinations: the study of some bones such as the skull, sacrum, long bones, etc., allows to determine the stature, age, race, sex, probable diseases, and sometimes the cause of death;
- Biological tests: the discovery and identification of genetic markers in products of biological origin (blood, saliva, sperm) allows positive identification as secure as through fingerprints;
- Fingerprint examination: particularly important in submerged bodies;
- Blood stains for analysis;
- Acquired brands: scars, pathological marks, professional marks, tattoos;
- Hands and feet must be protected with paper bags, for later collection of evidences;
- Clothing: preserve clothing;
- Personal adornments: wedding rings, breast medals, bracelets;
- Abnormally dressed clothing should be given special reference (a piece of clothing worn upside down makes it difficult to assess the facts);
- Clothes removed from the body should be cut by the seams or cut the buttons and undress the clothes without cutting them (ideal situation);
- Examination clothes/weapon go in individual packages (check each item); wet clothing, with blood or other fluids, should never be placed in plastic bags (decay makes observation, measurements and other examination steps difficult).

Mass disasters

During any local crime investigation, the safety of personnel and the preservation of life have the highest priority and are paramount with regard to the initial management of the crime scene. Emergency assistance must be given taking into account the needs of forensic science, but without compromising the absolute priority of victims. In this way, if the emergency teams arrive at the scene where a mass disaster occurred before the police, the team must immediately request their presence.

When arriving at the scene, the professionals must anticipate the indication of where the ambulances and other rescue vehicles should park. These sites should constitute areas that allow immediate access to victims. The parking areas may be far from the epicenter where the victims are, so there may be a need to transport the teams to the scene, as well as their equipment. In situations where units are directed to the crime scene area, care must be taken to avoid the presence of footprints, tire tracks, broken glass, and items such as cartridges when using firearms.

Entrances and exits: the movement should not prevent teams from being aware of the environment that surrounds them. Teams must remain vigilant for unknown material, collapses, damaged containers. Changing the direction of the entry point may be mandatory, requiring movement to be limited and to refocus on the location of the victims. In doing so, safety precautions are enhanced and will help professionals to remain aware of the responsibility to maintain attention.

Bodies and other large objects must not be moved unless they prevent the victims from being served. If it becomes imperative to move an object, you must report its original position. If the victim is obviously considered a body, it is appropriate for the emergency team to approach the next victims. In multiple victim scenarios, those that are considered "obviously dead," confirmation of asystole or any other manipulation of the body should not be performed. If it is really necessary, to confirm the death of the ECG, then this confirmation must be made with a minimum of body movement.

When entering chaotic scenes, teams must enter and leave the same path and leave the scene in its original condition. Entry must also be made with the minimum number of rescuers necessary to care for and recover the victims, and the route must be as direct as possible, to minimize contamination and alteration. Designating a path will limit the movements of rescuers and avoid unnecessary contact with the environment outside the treatment area. In cases where the police police arrives before the emergency teams, the first may have already designated an entry path, which the teams must respect, if it does not compromise the rescue and rescue of the victims.

Personal protective equipment will protect health care professionals from contamination with body fluids, but also the scene, preventing health care professionals from leaving their DNA in areas where investigators may have to perform the forensic examination. It is also imperative that emergency personnel do not enter directly into places where there are pools of blood or other fluids.

Many emergency teams use in their protocols the definition of what is considered "obvious death":

- Decapitation
- Incineration of 90% or more of the total body surface area
- Decomposition or putrefaction
- Transection of the thorax
- Total incineration of the victim's torso or head
- Cadaveric rigidity
- Total separation of vital organs from the body or total destruction of these organs accompanied by undetectable pulse or breathing, and any other injury not compatible with life in an apneic victim without pulse.

Clothing and victim's estate: teams should avoid cutting any holes in clothing that may be related to the event. This protects against possible loss of evidence of stains or dust residue and other chemicals around the openings. Ideally, as little clothing as possible should be removed, this will also minimize the loss of valuable evidence. When removal of clothing becomes clinically necessary, professionals should do everything possible to retain the articles in paper bags. Bloody clothes should never be rolled up and placed in plastic bags. It is important that these bags be labeled with the case number.

Personal items and clothes should remain with the police authority. Most personal items will not be transported with the victim, especially when they come from an explosion scene (these are now evidence). When firearms are present, the hands of victims should not be cleaned, but rather bagged in paper bags.

The change of location may include items left behind. Medical teams may find it difficult to manage the waste produced during urgent procedures. A good rule is not to remove medical waste, except for puncture wounds. Investigators prefer that most medical waste remain to determine where victims were treated and what treatment was performed.

Documentation

Medical documentation within crime scenes is considered an important step in proper scene processing. As discussed earlier, it is acceptable to move some items when arriving around the victim; however, teams should make a clear note of what has been done to alter the area of the scene. The purpose of documentation in these situations is to create a visual record to help criminal investigators recreate an accurate picture of what occurred at the scene. This record will help preserve the location and relationship of evidence and physical conditions on the scene.

In these cases of mass disasters, the documentation also plays an important role in verifying the death of the victims and in recording the procedures that were carried out. It is also important to record the odors experienced at the scene.

Considerations on preservation of evidences

The performance of the medical team in the prehospital environment, in general, should frame these considerations:

1. Protect yourself and the rest of the rescue team. If there are no safety conditions, you should not enter the scene. As soon as you are safe, you should approach the victim and provide medical assistance.
2. Note on the medical record the time of activation and arrival at the scene.
3. Do not touch or move anything in the place, unless it is really necessary to assist the victim.
4. All emergency elements should enter and exit through the same place, avoiding to step or walk over fluids that are on the ground.
5. Observe and document the original location of the items before moving them (ideally, make a photographic record).
6. When removing the victim's clothes, leave them intact whenever possible. When it is necessary to cut the clothes, this should not be done through the existing holes, but through the seams.

7. Put the dry clothes in paper bags; if damp, put them in plastic bags, but do not close them.
8. Record the presence/absence of clothing and personal objects that are relevant.
9. If any object is removed from the scene, its action must be documented and the police informed.
10. Do not jeopardize the assistance to the victim in order to preserve evidences.
11. Document the treatments performed to the victim before the verification of death (if they have occurred), including the substances administered and techniques performed.
12. If the victim is already dead, not to touch the body.
13. As soon as the death is verified, the police should be contacted immediately.
14. In case of a traffic accident, preserve the place by parking the car outside the skid marks and braking.
15. In victims of violent death, paper bags should always be placed in the hands.
16. Isolate the place and keep all unnecessary people away from the scene.
17. Do not smoke or drink on the scene.
18. Identify the places of venous puncture and drainage, with circles (using a permanent pen).
19. Pay attention to the time of death record on the death verification document.
20. Record the characteristics of the environment that may be relevant (odors, lighting, temperature, etc.).
21. Wear personal protective equipment, to collect evidences.
22. Record all preserved and collected evidences, handing this record over to the police.
23. All envelopes and containers must be sealed, dated, and signed.

Considerations on evidence collection

Evidence collection can become a major problem in emergency situations, since the absolute priority is medical care for the victim. As previously stated, protective equipment (mask, gown and gloves) should be worn in order to avoid cross contamination. Each item must be individually packaged, sealed, and identified, thus maintaining the chain of custody of the evidence.

Vestiges	Examples	Collection methods
Body fluids	Blood, urine, gastric content, and semen	• Collection of fluids by swab absorption; • In case of large quantities of fluids, aspirate with a syringe and place in a dry tube; • Gastric content: collect from the gastric bag or if it was aspirated with a vacuum cleaner, remove from the aspiration bag and place in a dry tube; • Allow the swab to air dry, place in an envelope, seal and identify.
Hair and fiber	Hair, carpet fibers	• Collect with tweezers and place in an envelope. Seal and identify; • If the hair is attached to a blood, metal or glass stain, it must be marked with a permanent pen, wrapped and placed in an envelope; • If it is difficult to collect, use tape and place on paper.
Fragments	Glass, paint, wood, plant material	Collect and separate in paper envelopes.
Waste	Gunpowder, GSR in the victim's hands	• Collect the material in clothing or in places where residues are present; • Put paper bags in the victim's hands.

Vestiges	Examples	Collection methods
Tooth brands	Any part of the body	Before washing or disinfecting the wound area, you should: • Pass moist swab (sterile water) on the area; • Allow to air dry, put in an envelope, seal and identify.
Strange bodies	Bullets, knives	• Handle as little as possible; • Do not try to clean the bullets. Allow to air dry and place in urine bottle; • Weapons (pistol, knife, etc.) must be placed in a cutting container and handed over to the authority.
Clothing	CLOTHES	• Carefully remove the garments as soon as possible. If it is not possible to undress, cut at the seams; • Wet clothing must be dried outdoors. If it is not possible to dry the clothes, wrap them in paper and put them in a plastic bag, but without closing it; • Separate clothing by pieces and store individually; • Preferably, put the clothes in paper bags; • Do not put your clothes on the floor, but on a white sheet; • Place the shoes individually in paper bags; • Seal the bags and identify.

After the preservation and evidence collection phase is completed, the body must be deposited in an appropriate transport bag (body bag), closed so that nothing is lost during transport. The bag must be placed in a rigid structure, so that there is no damage to the body. Along with the body, all available information on the case must be sent: death verification sheet, observation form, photographs, body diagrams, and collected evidences.

CHAPTER 11

Forensic artifacts

Cardiopulmonary resuscitation is an emergency procedure involving external chest compression and artificial ventilation, aiming to restore the flow of oxygenated blood to the brain and heart, in individuals with cardiac arrest. Its relative simplicity allows resuscitation to be performed both in the prehospital environment and in the hospital environment.

Resuscitation complications can create unusual injuries, which the forensic pathologist must be aware of, to prevent them from being misinterpreted. In this chapter, we intend to demonstrate the scope of the injuries that can be found during the medicolegal autopsy, and that can complicate the forensic assessment of cases, to determine the cause of death.

Head and neck

Wounds related to resuscitation can be seen by performing a physical examination. Bruises and abrasions can be seen on the scalp and face. The use of a resuscitation mask can injure us in the soft tissues of the nose, as well as the action of maintaining a permeable airway can result in abrasions in the mandible region caused by the nails. These marks can lead to misinterpretations of strangulation. However, the distribution and pattern are generally different, except for abrasions produced when checking the carotid pulse.

Injuries to the face can follow the removal of vomit. Inside the mouth, wounds in the mucosa surrounding the lips can occur, using the Guedel tube. There may also be damage to teeth and lips due to intubation or insertion of an oropharyngeal airway. The use of the nasopharyngeal tube has been associated with damage to the nasal passages, including the turbinates. Esophageal intubation can result in perforation of the esophagus.

EMS in Crime Scene. DOI: https://doi.org/10.1016/B978-0-12-824420-3.00014-9

Some studies have linked the appearance of retinal hemorrhage in children who have undergone cardiac compression maneuvers. The authors say that the chest pressure created during cardiac compression can lead to retinal hemorrhage. Forensic pathologists should therefore pay special attention to the investigation of these cases and the interpretation of retinal lesions. The presence of deep bleeding can be seen in the neck due to the insertion of central venous lines. In cases of orotracheal intubation, wounds of the mucosa of the larynx as well as contusions at the base of the tongue, these wounds can simulate inflicted injuries caused by compression of the neck. Laryngeal fractures (hyoid bone and thyroid cartilage), although reported, seem to constitute a rare complication of resuscitation and intubation.

Deep hemorrhage maybe seen in the neck from the insertion of central venous line. Mucosal injuries of the larynx can occur as well as contusions from the base of the tongue to the oropharynx such that resuscitation intubation that may simulate inflicted injuries caused by neck compressions.

Edema of pharyngeal structures may result from the use of laryngeal mask. Hemorrhage can be an immediate complication of emergency tracheostomy.

Chest

The areas where external compression was applied may show abrasions/contusions. Also, the areas where defibrillation was applied can show abrasion and burn. Electrical burns can occur from external pacing. In the chest, there may be incisions from the insertion of the drain or puncture marks through the use of needles to decompress a pneumothorax or emergency pericardiocentesis.

Rib and sternum fractures are the most common fractures found in resuscitated patients. Rib fractures can contribute to death, causing pneumothorax or cardiac lacerations. Myocardial hemorrhages attributed to the effects of heart compression may be present in the septum and in the region of the bundle of His. Laceration of the heart and pericardial sac can result from fractures of the ribs. Laceration of the pleural surface of the lungs can result from fractures of the ribs.

Distinguishing between primary (arrest causing) and secondary (caused by resuscitation), pathology can be difficult, and reliance may have to be placed on the history in addition to the findings.

Pulmonary fat embolism was found histologically in 81% of patients who received external cardiac massage.

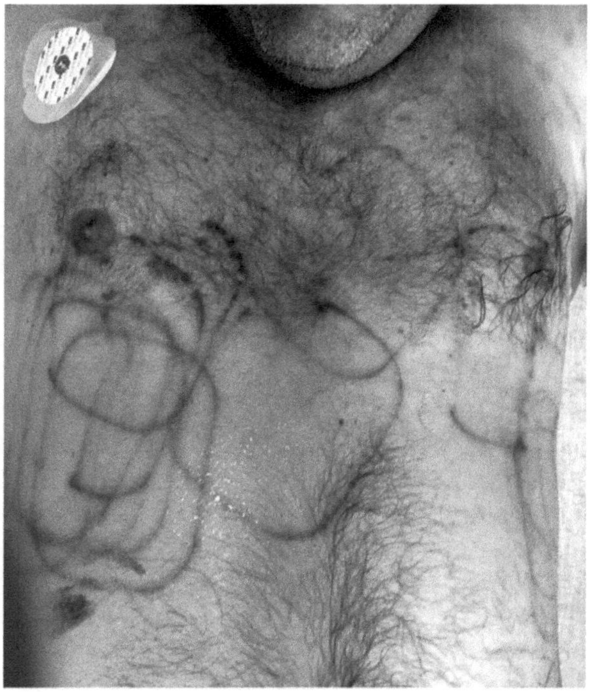

Picture 1—Defibrillation injuries.

Abdomen and peritoneum retro

Incorrect hand placement on the xiphoid appendix of the sternum during cardiopulmonary resuscitation can increase the likelihood of visceral injuries. Abnormalities of the spleen or liver can contribute to an increased risk of laceration. Mouth-to-mouth ventilation or the use of a manual insufflator with a mask can create gastric distention and promote gastric rupture, which must be differentiated from gastromalacia. Children may be more vulnerable to liver damage during resuscitation, due to the relatively small size of the pediatric chest.

Skin and subcutaneous injuries

Bruising around wounds by intravenous puncture on the hands and feet is common and substantial and can also form bruises. The medical team can circle these wounds with pens to help pathologists differentiate them from preexisting needle punctures.

Manual versus resuscitation only device assisted

There are three different main categories of resuscitation: manual/traditional; manual/device-assisted (i.e., with a hand pump, to improve blood flow); and automated/device-assisted. In a comparison between standard cardiopulmonary resuscitation and active compression/decompression, there were more victims with bruised sternum in the active compression/decompression. In a study comparing traditional/manual cardiopulmonary resuscitation with the use of an automated band (Auto Pulse), rib fractures were statistically significantly more common in patients who had undergone manual resuscitation; however, a pattern of injury was found in the fractures that were caused by the Auto Pulse device. Visceral lesions were found with laceration of the right lobe of the liver, laceration of the mesenteric, and laceration of the spleen.

CHAPTER 12

911 call center

The emergency centers that receive emergency calls, be it the 911 call center or the emergency centers at firefighters, play a very important role not only in screening calls but also in predicting the severity of the call in relation to a possible forensic scenario. One of the most critical calls that emergency dispatchers answer concerns cases of interpersonal violence. In fact, operators receive the distress call from the suspect himself, without, however, knowing that it is him. There are few studies on this topic, but it is a topic of special interest, since it can help emergency teams, as well as police and criminal investigation, from the start of activation.

There is a study on emergency calls, in which eight indicators were identified associated with the prediction of the probability of innocence or guilt of those who called for help. These indicators, although not very frequent, are relevant for information, and to assist emergency operators to screen calls. The trend indicators consist of apologizing to the victim, asking for authorization, calling another person, operating as a witness, commenting on the observation, an indicator of nervous laughter, having a problem, and retelling the dialog.

Apologizing to the victim

Some homicides occur when the aggressors lose their patience and attack the victims once they show a state of anger. Many cases of domestic violence and child abuse fit into this profile. Sometimes these attackers regret their actions and call 911 to ask for help. Although there is a will on the part of the aggressors that the victims live, they cannot divulge the whole truth to the emergency operators, because they are in a self-protection mode. Sometimes operators can hear the attackers apologizing to the victim(s) for what happened. This behavior alone is already suspect since an innocent person who calls 911 would not need to apologize for anything unless they were involved in the assault.

EMS in Crime Scene. DOI: https://doi.org/10.1016/B978-0-12-824420-3.00008-3

Requesting authorization to rescue

Innocent people who call 911 rarely ask operators for authorization to provide first aid to victims. In effect, they focus on the victims and take immediate measures to comfort and stabilize them. However, some people who are "guilty" ask emergency operators for consent to help victims. In the study carried out, the authorization request indicator was present in 5% of calls [54]. The "guilty" individuals made 89% of these calls and the "innocent" individuals made 11%. Some "guilty" individuals, in this same study, were passive when interacting with their loved ones who were seriously injured, asking timidly for authorization from the operator to help the victims.

Calling someone else

Innocent people who call 911 understand that time is critical when asking for help to help an injured person. Therefore after evaluating the situation as a life-threatening event, the first call should be to 911. Some people, however, made other calls before contacting 911. This indicator occurred at 4% of calls. All, except a call with this indicator, were made by "guilty" people.

Calling someone else before calling 911 means wasting time and reducing victims' chances of survival. A review of this practice revealed that it was a defensive strategy for the benefit of the aggressors. The attackers could give their own opinion about the events, being the first to hear about the incident.

In the study [54], calling someone else was used most often when a boyfriend or stepfather was taking care of a child, whereas the mother was away from home. After assaulting the child and seeing that the victim's condition was deteriorating, some abusers panicked and called the mother before calling 911, which gave the abusers an opportunity to explain to the mother before the police found out the truth.

In the second defensive strategy, the attackers sought the mother's advice and gave her enough time to get home before calling 911. When the police arrived on the scene, the attacker and the mother were seen as the medical team. In some cases, male abusers sent a text message to the mother before calling 911.

Emergency operator as a witness

Some attackers used the strategy of bringing the emergency operator as a witness to support their possible innocence. In this technique, the attackers narrated each step as they walked the scene with the operators in line as if they were discovering the victim for the first time.

The attackers also "discovered" entry points, weapons, and other evidence, while on the phone with emergency operators. In the study carried out, this indicator was present in 4% of the calls, and all but one were made by "guilty" people [54].

Observation comments

Innocent people focus on the victims' most serious injuries and quickly share this crucial information with operators. Some "guilty" people did not provide critical details and instead made, for example, comments about the victim's eyes, without this information being requested by the emergency operator. In the study, 6% of the calls contained comments about the victim's gaze. The attackers made 82% of these calls, whereas innocent people made only 18% [54].

Nervous laughter

There is nothing funny in potentially fatal situations. No innocent interlocutor in the study carried out, laughed, or had any moment of humor, when communicating with the emergency operators, while calling 112 to ask for help. However, 3% of study participants [54] laughed or found a joke, when answering questions from operators. In fact, they were all the aggressors. This behavior on the part of the aggressors (laugh, find joke) occurred when they finished their comments.

Having a problem

Several people who were guilty started their phone calls giving the impression that they were victims. These people revealed their problem using the singular personal pronoun "I" and started the conversation with: "I have a problem…"; for example: "I have a problem, I have a child who does not breathe"; "I have a problem, my wife disappeared."

Recount of the dialog

Put yourself in the shoes of someone who enters a place where a death occurred. The body is lifeless, possibly with huge injuries and severe bleeding. If the victim is a friend or a family member, the stress would be severe. So, the 911 call should convey that a person is in shock or nervous. The caller is expected to urgently call for help, because the focus is on the victim, and any information that delays the operator in activating the rescue means is counterproductive.

Some people, however, took the time to retell the dialog they had with the victim. This indicator was present in 6% of calls. The perpetrators made 82% of these calls, whereas innocent people made only 18% of the calls. In the study, it was concluded that the attackers used the dialog recount for three reasons:

1. to incriminate the victim and to gain sympathy from the emergency operators;
2. to present an alibi to the operator; and
3. to divert attention to another possible suspect.

The homicide calls that are made to the emergency center are unique. They occur on the part of people who are in difficulty, facing urgent situations of life and/or death. These initial telephone contacts contain invaluable statements, because they are called less edited by the suspect's attempt to hide the truth, they are not contaminated as the subsequent declarations may be, and they are also free from contamination of the interviewers' verbal and nonverbal behavior.

In fact, 911 calls are usually the only neat statements in the entire investigation. To ensure that the call to 911 is as pure as possible, emergency operators should use the open question: "911, what is your emergency?" Then, they should ask "What happened?" Callers can choose where their story begins. This freedom of choice empowers callers.

The willingness of 911 calls increases their investigative value. Whoever calls the emergency center initiates the conversation, thereby removing any questions regarding coercion. Who calls 911 and who is under great emotional stress usually provides more information than intended. This spontaneous information can provide critical clues and reveal details of events that precede death, such as fights or threats, as well as information about the death itself.

The voluntary words of the 911 caller may reveal the true motive for the murder. One of the main advantages of the statements made at 911 is that the dialog is recorded, allowing investigators to analyze the tone of voice, volume, rhythm, and tone of the caller. The location and duration of breaks in the conversation also provide clues as to the focus of the 911 caller. Criminal investigation teams should therefore request access to the 911 call recordings, as they may contain unique information. At the same time, emergency operators must be increasingly trained to detect the possible cases of interpersonal violence that can lead to homicide, and that requires special care by the emergency services that are activated for the location. If the team that is activated for the location already has information about the possibility of dealing with a forensic case, their approach can already be prepared and guided in another way.

CHAPTER 13

Documentation in forensic cases

The best way to protect the medical team, as well as the victim, is the perfect documentation of the facts, since in emergency situations it may be the only way to preserve evidences. In the records, some items must always be documented: the condition in which the victim is and the surrounding area; the treatment performed; the circumstances of the event.

Medicolegal documentation in forensic cases is critical. Thus the use of body diagrams should be used to determine the distribution of injuries. In addition to written notes, annotation of findings on a body diagram will be very useful for others who are determining the distribution and pattern of injuries. A body diagram does not need to be complex but should convey the location and type of injuries. The medical team must examine the patient and document, in the body diagram, what was found, describing the type of injury, its location, and the number of injuries. The victim's behavior and mental state should be noted. The registration must be accurate, complete, objective, and legible. When documenting injuries, care should be taken to describe them according to the anatomical plane, separating the left side from the right. In situations of aggression with a firearm, the caliber of ammunition should not be described (the description of the caliber can lead to the investigation of misconceptions), but only the entrance and exit orifices (if any and if identified).

There are many reasons for the lack of appropriate charting. Failure of documentation results from lack of clinical independence, inadequate training, economic and other pressures, excessive workload, physical and psychological pressures, lack of body diagrams on which to make notes, lack of photographic equipment, and lack of awareness.

Expressions should not be described in the notes as is the case of "allegedly." Effectively, health professionals do not "claim" that someone has chest pain.

EMS in Crime Scene. DOI: https://doi.org/10.1016/B978-0-12-824420-3.00006-X

It is important to follow the following suggestions to ensure your documentation holds up to intense scrutiny of many people, including personnel not familiar with clinical terminology (i.e., law enforcement). When writing in a narrative note, follow these rules:

- describe wounds in a logical sequence; for example, head to toe;
- use landmarks to identify areas of injury. Good ones include the midline of the body, the notch at the top of the breastbone, the centerline of a limb, the heel, and the external ear canals.

Victims of violent crime must remain isolated in the living room/bedroom, with limited access for people. All visits must be identified and registered. The medical team in the prehospital must make the following records:

- identification (if possible)
- physical description of the victim
- last words, if you spoke to the team
- personal history and treatment
- description of the location found—ventilation, light, temperature, humidity, odor conditions, body position and condition, clothes, and possible movements
- signs of death, due to the cessation of vital functions—respiratory, circulatory, and nervous
- diagnostic/therapeutic maneuvers performed, as well as possible changes to the scene, due to these maneuvers
- signs of death due to the establishment of cadaverous phenomena

When dealing with stab wounds and bullet holes

- measure to the center of the wound;
- do not measure the location of one injury in relation to another (unless the injuries are obviously paired like the tines on a fork);
- do not disperse or split parts of a single injury into more than one measurement.

When describing marks that encircle or partially encircle the wrists, ankles, or neck, begin with "For descriptive purposes, the marking commences at point."

Remember that you must document the location, size, and appearance/character of defects before they are altered by the passage of time or medical interventions.

The importance of accurate reporting

It is common to see that the reports of the medical teams are absent from the statements of the main players in the area. In fact, the suspect may be on the scene, and the medical team may not be aware of this situation. At the same time, an individual who appears to be an innocent party may actually be the aggressor.

In homicide cases, it may happen that the victim is still alive but dies soon after. Any word from the victim can be very important. When documenting statements made by people on the scene, it is important to quote them as accurately as possible and enclose your observations in quotes to show that they are statements and not interpretations.

Signs of death—corneal opacity, sclerotic black spot, livores—distribution; coloring and fixation; cooling of the face, neck, hands, feet, and covered parts; stiffness of the jaw, face, neck, trunk, upper limbs, and lower limbs.

The daily reality of the teams shows that, normally, victims are usually occupied in providing care and that the notes are written later, making it difficult to reconstruct what was said. I can describe a case in which the emergency medical services (EMS) team documented what was said on the spot and how it helped with the conviction. A 16-month-old baby died of hypothermia in a bathtub. No marks were found on the body. There was no evidence of abuse. When EMS arrived at the scene, the babysitter said that she had just put the baby in the bath and that the water was hot and that she had gone to another room for a moment to prevent two other children from being beaten. When she returned, the victim was submerged in the water. She said she pulled her out, started CPR, and called 911 immediately. In the hospital, the baby's core temperature was 26°C. Criminal Investigators talked to the babysitter, and she changed her story in relation to what she had said to the EMS team, and which had been documented. If the EMS team had not written the statements, the babysitter would have changed the story and the criminal investigation would have had a harder time investigating the case.

Fact versus truth

An important concept of documentation is to record the facts, not the truth. A fact is objective, the truth is a judgment or a conclusion. For example, calling a wound "self-inflicted" is a judgment, unless you can support the claim by documenting the victim's or witnesses' statements. Another pitfall for teams occurs when it is documented that a person is "drunk" or "intoxicated," it is also a judgment or conclusion. Therefore one should document only the facts and let the reader reach a conclusion.

Calls involving possible cases of child, domestic, and elder abuse can be difficult to prove or disprove, but an accurate report can be very important in these legal cases. This is where objectivity becomes crucial, and accurate documentation of all injuries must be made, including location, size, shape, and color. It is also important to document what other witnesses say about what happened, as well as what the patient says and their behavior and way of acting. It should be noted what was seen and heard, but not to interpret what it means. In fact, if trials are included, you may end up being questioned by a defense attorney for a period of 30 minutes about your training and experience.

It is essential to note and document the following in crime scenarios:

1. evidence of forced entry
2. layout of the room where the victim is
3. location of the victim
4. location of weapons or potential weapons
5. signs of struggle
6. ammunition and capsules
7. tire brands
8. lights (off/on)
9. curtains (closed/open)
10. TVs, radios (on/off)
11. position of furniture

In relation to the victim, the following must be documented:

1. position and location
2. mental state
3. evidence of intoxication
4. evidence of injuries
5. evidence of sexual abuse

6. testimony made by the victim
7. declarations of death
8. containment marks
9. location of injuries and burns
10. presence of damage to clothing

Important points for documenting

For documentation to be effective, consider the following:

Chain of custody begins with whoever collected the evidence and must be maintained on all specimens. If you do not have chain of custody tags, you can obtain them from your local police crime laboratory or various forensic-oriented websites. Often, the police will bring tags with them when they come to collect the evidence you have gathered. To ensure the chain of custody is as short as possible, one health care professional should manage the patient.

The patient's history and examination findings should be exact and detailed to avoid any misinterpretation. Events of the incident should be detailed enough to determine the quality of the complaint and the extent of the examination. Remember, chart objectively. If the patient says anything to you, document it exactly and in quotation marks.

The health care provider examines the patient and documents the findings on the figures in the progress notes. Describe the injury type, location, and number in as much detail as possible. Draw pictures, if needed, to depict injuries accurately (a body diagram helps depict injuries pictorially). The mental state of the patient should be noted. In addition, the condition of the patient's clothing should be noted.

Sometimes, you will transfer evidence to a law enforcement official. It is critical to document this in your EMS notes. A suggested statement includes: "[Patient name] [medical record number], specific items [including blood tubes, gastric contents, personal belongings], was conveyed from [your name] to the criminal investigator [name] on [date] at [time]."

Photo-documentation

The photo-documentation of injuries and wounds is a standard procedure, and extremely important, for the investigation and for the victim.

Photography requires consent from the victim and is a part of the investigation process. There are injuries that are difficult to describe, so photo-documentation should be used in these situations [15].

The objectives of photography are as follows [53]:

- record and communicate what cannot be communicated by words;
- serve as a testimony, with the aim of providing photos for judgment;
- protect health professionals against allegations of inadequate care or lack of documentary accuracy, physical appearance, condition, or injuries;
- record and document injuries and evidences that cannot be preserved for a long time;
- to be used as a future memory;
- registration of injuries that will be changed with medical procedures;
- allow the court to view wounds;
- document wounds and conditions, before and after the treatment;
- demonstrate intentionality;
- demonstrate the absence of wounds;
- illustrate and supplement the written record;
- training of professionals and students.

Photographs must be taken from the same angle, with the same scale. In case there is no scale rule, a pen, a coin can be used for size reference [53]. A photograph should be taken showing the body in relation to the location to give an indication of its framing. Attach the victim's name (if known), date, location, and identification of who took the photo. Photographs must be placed in an envelope, sealed, and labeled. The number of photographs taken of the patient should be documented [53].

Rules

- photograph all wounds before and after treatment/disinfection. It is important for recording blood splashes, gunpowder residues;
- place a tag with the victim's data next to the wound to photograph;
- take a full-body photograph, capturing both the face and the lesions, to highlight the trauma and allow the victim to be identified. Also, take a full-body photograph with the victim on his back, with his head turned toward the camera. Objectively, the intention is to register the presence or absence of wounds;
- respect the victim's privacy. Allow the victim to cover themselves with a blanket or sheet, move it only to expose areas and injuries that need to be photographed;

- perform the photograph essentially in four anatomical positions: anterior, posterior, right side, and left side;
- take pictures with zoom of each wound and take pictures with and without scale;
- identify each photograph with date and time, hospital name/EMS, emergency episode, photographer's name, and place in a sealed envelope. Photos must accompany the victim's file.

Photographing injuries

Photo-documentation is an effective way to preserve the appearance of the wounds as noted by the examiner on a given day. Remember that wounds heal and may look entirely different hours or days later. Most of you have heard the age-old saying that a "picture is worth a thousand words." Photographs of all body surfaces can quite effectively illustrate his condition when he arrived at the hospital.

Get a full-length picture of the patient's body and face, and a close-up of each injury. Use a photographic scale or ruler; if no scale is available, use a coin or other common object as a size reference. Document the photograph according to hospital policy and link it carefully to the photographs of specific wounds. Label the photograph with the patient's name, medical record number, and the date and time of the photograph. Consider taking two sets of photographs (one for medical records and one for law enforcement).

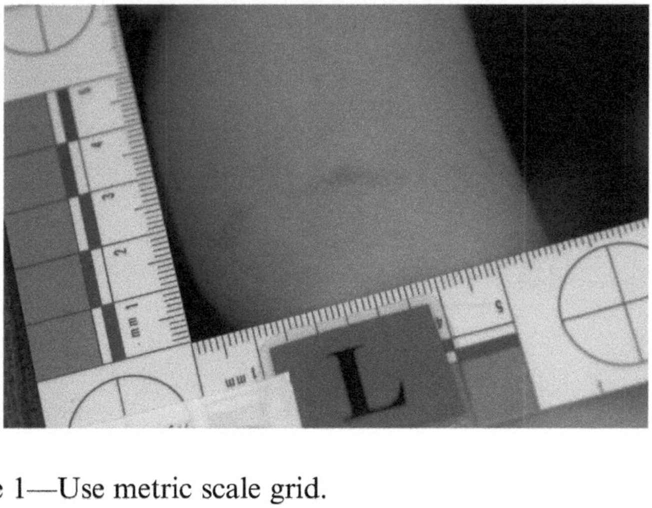

Picture 1—Use metric scale grid.

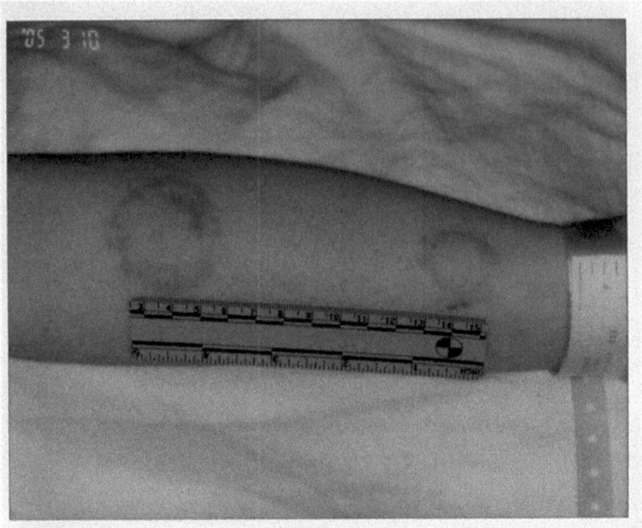

Picture 2—Metric position for distance reference between wounds.

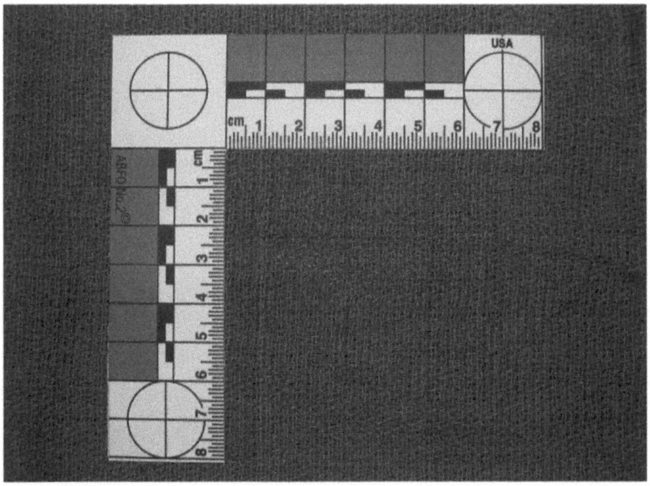

Picture 3—Reference metric scale.

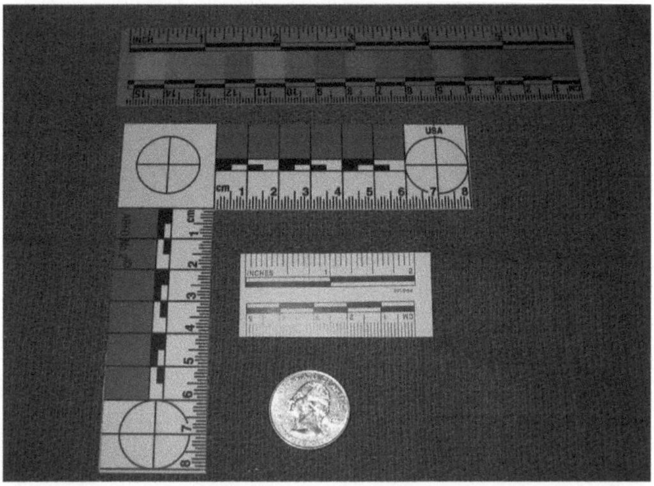

Picture 4—Different metric scales.

Picture 1 + 2 + 3 + 4

This is the best way to photograph a wound for medicolegal purposes. Using a grayscale ruler helps to ensure the photo is developed properly. If you do not have something like this available, use a coin as a size reference for investigators.

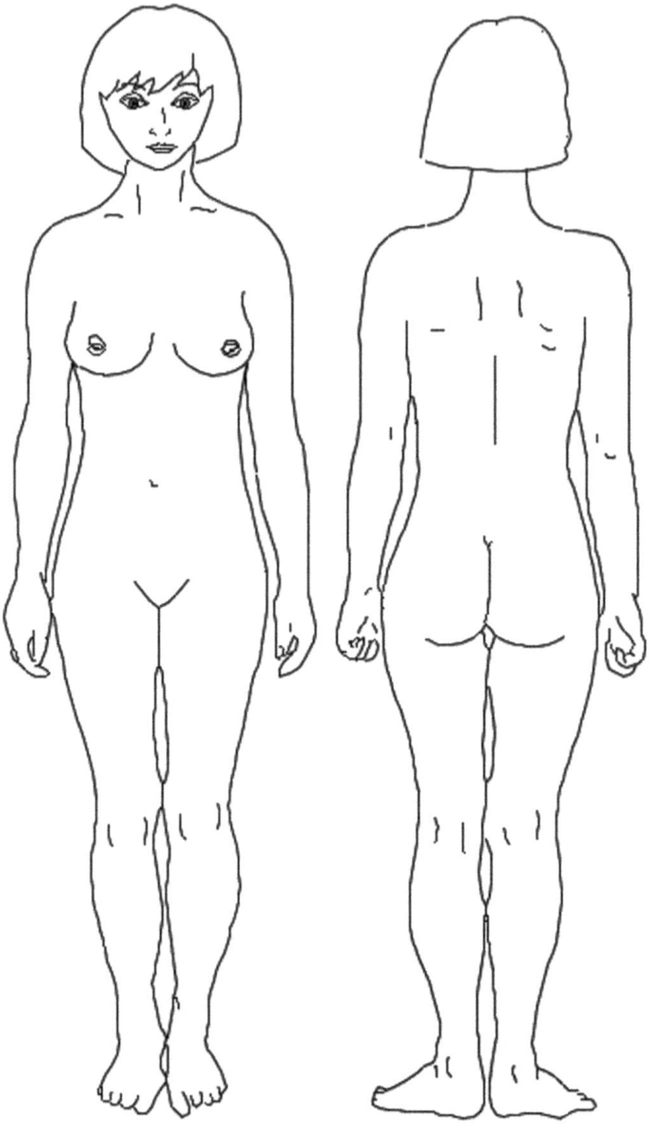

Picture 5—Female body diagram.

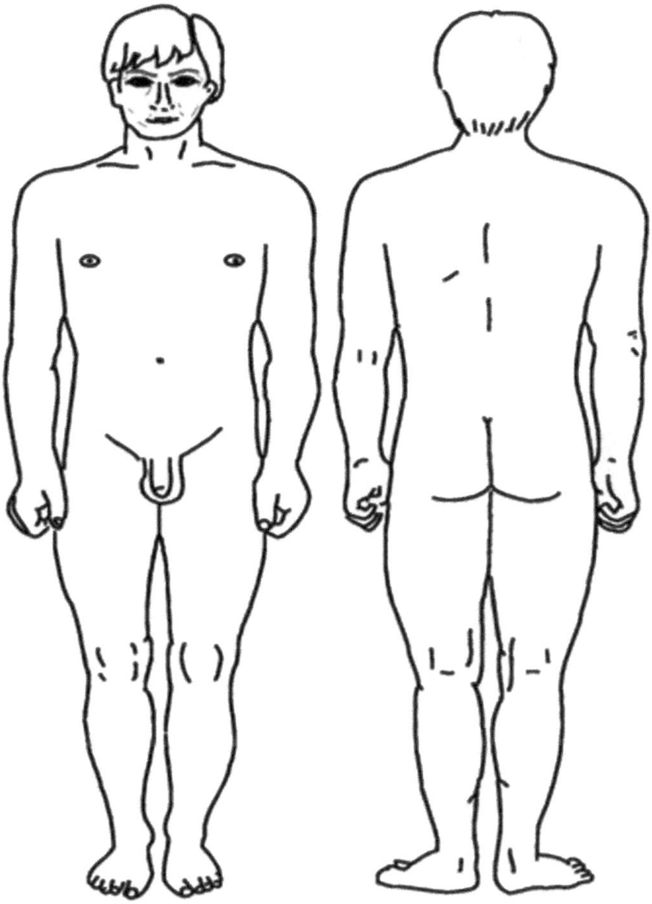

Picture 6—Male body diagram.

CHAPTER 14

Intra- and extra-hospital material for preservation and collection of evidences

It is intended, in this chapter, to propose a list of materials that can constitute a suitcase for preservation and collection of evidences. This list is identical for the intra- and extra-hospital environment since the situations that occur are also identical.

Material for preserving and collecting evidences:

- tweezers
- mirror
- nylon brush
- containers
- scissors
- spatulas
- protection masks
- envelopes of various sizes
- gloves
- scalpel blades
- smocks
- protective goggles
- cotton balls
- permanent pen
- cotton swabs
- ruler
- filter paper
- adhesive
- distilled water
- paper bags of various sizes
- dry tubes
- camera (plus memory cards, backup battery, remote flash, tripod, and remote cord)
- pipettes

EMS in Crime Scene. DOI: https://doi.org/10.1016/B978-0-12-824420-3.00007-1

- syringes
- sterile compresses
- white self-adhesive labels
- chalk
- bindle paper
- biohazard bags
- crime scene barricade tape
- flares
- flashlight and extra batteries
- markers (e.g., business cards, chalk, spray paint, or some other marker to place by noted evidence items)
- notebook
- personal protective equipment (e.g., gloves, booties, hair covering, overalls, and mask)
- evidence seals/tape
- measuring devices (e.g., measuring wheel, tape measures of varying lengths).
- reflective vest

This list is only for the police. Officers may need to use other items and may wish to have them readily available in their police vehicle. These items include

- audio recorder
- biohazard labels
- bloodstain pattern examination kit
- business cards
- backup camera
- chalk
- cutting instruments (knives, box cutter, scalpel, scissors)
- directional marker/compass
- disinfectant
- distilled water
- entomology (insect) collection kit
- evidence collection containers (e.g., jars, paper bags, resealable plastic bags, metal paint style cans)
- evidence identifiers
- evidence seals/tape
- extension cords
- fingerprint ink pad and pint cards for elimination prints

- flags (surveyor type) for marking evidence and setting up search patterns
- forensic light source (alternate light source, UV lamp/laser, goggles)
- generator
- gunshot residue kit
- high-intensity lights
- labels
- laser trajectory kit
- magnifying glass
- maps
- marker stickers such as numbers, letters, arrows, scales
- marking paint/snow wax
- metal detector
- mirror
- nail clippers and orange peeler (for collecting debris under suspect fingernails)
- phone listing (important numbers)
- pocket knife
- presumptive blood test supplies
- privacy screens
- protrusion rod set
- rakes
- razor blades or knife (knife must have blades that can be broken off after each use)
- reflective vest
- refrigeration or cooling unit
- respirators with filters
- roll of string
- rubber bands
- screen sifters
- sexual assault evidence collection kit (for victim and suspect)
- shoe print lifting equipment
- tarps to protect evidence from the weather
- templates (scene and human)
- thermometer
- tool kit
- traffic cones
- trajectory rods
- waterless hand wash (towelette with germicide)

Examples of evidence collection kits

A blood collection kit might include
- bindle
- coin envelopes
- disposable scalpels
- distilled water
- ethanol
- evidence identifiers
- latex gloves
- photographic ruler (ABFO scales)
- presumptive chemicals
- sterile gauze
- sterile swabs
- test tubes/test tube rack

A bloodstain pattern documentation kit might include
- ABFO scales
- calculator
- laser pointer
- permanent markers
- protractor
- string
- tape

An excavation kit might include
- cones/markers
- evidence identifiers
- metal detectors
- paintbrushes
- shovels/trowels
- sifting screens
- string
- weights
- wooden/metal stakes

A fingerprint kit might include
- black and white film
- brushes
- chemical enhancement supplies
- cyanoacrylate (super glue) wand/packets
- flashlight
- forensic light source

- lift cards
- lift tape
- measurement scales
- one-to-one camera
- powders

An impression kit might include

- impression
- bowls/mixing containers
- boxes
- dental stone (die stone)
- evidence identifiers
- measurement scales
- permanent markers
- snow print wax
- water

A pattern print lifter kit might include

- casting materials (casting material, distilled water if needed for casting material, casting frames, mixing bowl if needed for casting material, polymer type casting material with various size spreader tips.)
- chemical enhancement supplies
- electrostatic dust lifter
- gel lifter
- wide-format lift tape

A trace evidence collection kit might include

- acetate sheet protectors
- bindle paper
- clear tape/adhesive lift
- electrostatic dust lifter
- flashlight (oblique lighting)
- forceps/tweezers
- glass vials
- slides and slide mailers
- trace evidence vacuum with disposable collection filters

A trajectory kit might include

- calculator
- canned smoke
- dummy

- laser
- mirror
- protractor
- string
- trajectory rods

CHAPTER 15

Final considerations

Prehospital emergency teams are usually the first to arrive at the place where a forensic event occurred. As such, they must be prepared to at least minimize the possibility of contamination and destruction of traces that may be essential for criminal investigation teams to carry out their work. It is of particular importance to document everything that involves the event, but mainly what concerns the victim's body and the circumstances surrounding the death.

This book aims to help health professionals who work in prehospital teams, as well as all those who work in the hospital, on how they can preserve and collect evidences in the face of forensic situations that require special attention and care. Obviously, the basis of the approach to victims of violent death is essentially based on the common sense of each professional, on the recognition and identification of potential victims, on the preservation of evidences, and on the subsequent report to the judicial entities. Maintaining the chain of custody is also essential so that an evidence is considered valid for the investigation of the case.

Health professionals should not be policemen or investigators. In fact, that is not their role, but they should report anything that is suspicious. The collection of history is of vital importance, since it can lead to the reconstruction of the event. Physical examination is also essential, as it allows the health professionals to be able to identify suspicious injuries, as well as the place where evidences that may corroborate the suspicion can be collected.

Professionals working in the prehospital must carefully observe the location of the event, since it may contain unique evidences that can change over time and with the presence of several stakeholders. For example, the presence of any odor in the place must be documented immediately, because hours or minutes later, it may have disappeared. Likewise, if they need to change the scene to help the victim, they

EMS in Crime Scene. DOI: https://doi.org/10.1016/B978-0-12-824420-3.00001-0

must document the respective changes that have been made, because otherwise, it may interfere with the investigation of the case.

The premise of Locard must always be present in the minds of all those who are at the crime scene that when entering a scene, the individual brings with him traces that he will leave there, just as when he leaves the scene, he will take with him evidences of it. When remembered, this premise will cause the participants to take universal measures of protection (gown, gloves, mask), as well as to control the scene, not allowing the participants to move freely through it and contaminate it. Teams must not smoke, eat, and drink on scene and preferably should only have a single entry and exit. Whenever possible, they should try not to step on any fluids that may be on scene.

Legal issues

You may be called to treat terminally ill patients. Legally the patient has a right to refuse resuscitative efforts. For this situation is necessary an advance directive, that is instructions written in advance. This document is signed by the patient against resuscitation. Three types of advance directives are a DO NOT Resuscitate (DNR) order, a living will and a health care proxy. A DNR is a legal document or order that most often governs resuscitation issues only. A living will is more often used to cover more general health care issues. A health care proxy is a person who is legally designated if he is unable to do so for himself.

Under the law the patient has the right to accept or refuse emergency medical care. Therefore it is necessary to obtain consent, or permission, before providing such care. Before emergency care is rendered the patient must be informed of the care to be provided and the consequences and risks. Consent so obtained is termed informed consent. If you were to touch a patients body or clothing without first obtaining the proper consent, you can be charged with assault and battery. There are three types of consent: expressed consent, implied consent (when you assume that a patient who is unresponsive, would consent to life-saving emergency care) and minor consent (consent for a minor or mentally incompetent adult).

Under the law, to refuse treatment or transport a patient must be informed and fully understand the treatment and all risks and consequences of refusal. Once this been accomplished, you must require that the patient sign an official "release from liability" form.

Other legal aspects of emergency care

Abandonment and negligence

There are two different situations in which an EMS may be held legally liable for decisions made in the course of treatment: abandonment and negligence. Abandonment means that you stopped providing care without ensuring that equivalent or better care would be provided. Under abandonment laws, once you start giving emergency care to a patient, you must continue until another health care professional takes over care.

You may be considered negligent by law if the care you provide deviates from the accepted standard of care and results in further injury to the patient.

Confidentiality

Do not speak to the press, your family, friends or other members of the public about details of the emergency care you provided to a patient. Releasing confidential information requires a written release form signed by the patient or a legal guardian.

REFERENCES

[1] A. Batuca, Representações sociais sobre o sistema integrado de emergência médica, Universidade católica Portuguesa, Faculdade de Ciências Humanas, Lisboa, 1998. Dissertação de mestrado em ciências de enfermagem.

[2] J.M. Fontanella, B. Chavagnac, Références Historiques de Láide Médicale Urgente Préhospitalière, in: J.M. Fontanella, et al. (Eds.), Les Samu- centre 15, Organisation activités techniques de régulation médicale- Eléments historiques, Sfem Editions-Collection Médecine d'Urgence Samu, Paris, 1998.

[3] H. Lee, C. Ladd, Preservation and collection of biological evidence, Croatian Med. J. 42 (3) (2001) 225–228.

[4] JR; DH G - Crime scene protection; FBI Law enforcement bulletin; September 1994 K. Olds, et al., Injuries associated with resuscitation, J. Forensic Legal Med. 33 (2015) 39–43.

[5] J. Horswell (Ed.), The Practice of Crime Scene Investigation, CRC Press LLC, USA, 2004.

[6] C. Chahestian, D. Zaki, Atendimento Pré-hospitalar; Rio de Janeiro: 2004. III Simpósio de Emergência do Hospital de Santa Catarina. [consultado em 19-05-2011]. Disponível em URL: <www.hsc.org.br/simpósio/APH1_arquivos/slide0053.htm>.

[7] T. Gonçalves, Funcionamento e meios de um SIEM. INEM, Lisboa: Ano II, n°5, 1986.

[8] LEI n° 45/2004 de 19 de agosto, Estabelece o regime jurídico das perícias médico-legais e forenses, 2004.

[9] R. Rosas, Fundamentos de balistica en heridas ocasionadas por proyecteis de arma de fuego, Trauma 14 (3) (2001) 115–120. Septiembre/Diciembre.

[10] J. Lello, E. Lello (Eds.), Dicionário prático ilustrado, Lello, Porto, 1995.

[11] E. Locard, A investigação criminal e os métodos científicos, Coimbra Editora, Coimbra, 1939.

[12] B. Epstein, J. Maiuri, Levantamiento del cadáver, Facultad de Medicina, Catedral y Depto. De Medicina Legal, maio de 1997.

[13] R.J.S. Armas, Signos de la muerte (consultada em 16 de Dezembro 2009). Disponivel em: <http://agenciabk.net/BK86.htm>.

[14] G. França, Medicina Legal. Rio Janeiro: Guanabara, 1998.

[15] A. Gomes, Enfermagem forense, Vol. 2, Lidel, Lisboa, 2014.

[16] G. Calabuig, Medicina Legal y Toxicologia, 6th Edition, Masson, Barcelona, 2004.

[17] L. Rodrigues, A. Ginó, C. Sena, K. Dahlin, et al., Compreender os recursos humanos do Serviço Nacional de Saúde, Colibri; Apifarma, Lisboa, 2002.

[18] V. Di Maio, Gunshot Wounds: Practical Aspects of Firearms, Ballistics and Forensic Techniques, 2nd Edition, CRC Press LLC, New York, 1999.

[19] Technical Working Group on Crime Scene Investigation, Crime Scene Investigation: A Guide for Law Enforcement, US Department of Justice Office of Justice Programs, USA, 2000.

[20] A. Gomes, Enfermagem forense, Vol. 1, Lidel, Lisboa, 2014.

[21] L.N. Eliopulos, Death Investigator's Handbook, Paladin Express, USA, 1993.

[22] J. Wick, Don't destroy the evidence, AORN J. (2001) 1–13. Nov.

[23] L. Paiva, Patologia forense nas mortes com evidente ação do fogo; Saúde, ética e justiça (2006) 1–7.

[24] P. Safar, N. Bircher, Reanimacion cardiopulmonar y cerebral, Interamericana McGraw-Hill, Madrid, 1990.

[25] N. Paredes, D. Vélez, Cadena de Custodia: Una Obligación para el Professional de la Salud? Responsabilidad Juridica, Janero, 2006, pp. 24–26.

[26] Scene assessment, Manitoba Health Emergency Treatment Guidelines, August 2003, p. G3 – 1.

[27] E. Chenello, Ciência forense: manchas de sangre, Química virtual, janeiro, 2007, pp: 1–10.

[28] Larousse, Enciclopédia Visual e Temática. (s.l.): Seleções do Reader's Digest, 1995.

[29] D. Polit, Fundamentos em pesquisa em Enfermagem, Artes médicas, Porto Alegre, 1995.

[30] M.F.T. Pinheiro, Csi Criminal, Edições Universidade Fernando Pessoa, Porto, 2008.

[31] Universal, Dicionário Língua Portuguesa, Texto Editora, Lisboa, 2001.

[32] Direccion General de la Guardia Civil, Subdireccion General de Operaciones – Jefatura de Informacion y Policia Judicial – Manual de Policia Judicial. Madrid. 2000.

[33] F. Galvão, Preservação da Cadeia de Custódia em Vestígios Biológicos Forense (Dissertação de Mestrado), Faculdade de Medicina de Lisboa, 2006.

[34] Hospital of Saint Raphael, February NHSHP Crime Scene Guidelines, Hospital of Saint Raphael, Canada, 2007, pp. 2–4.

[35] J. Rando, V.R. Medina, Papel del médico forense en la inspeccion ocular y levantamiento del cadáver, Cuad. med. forense; Sevilha: Associacion de Médicos Forenses de Andalucía. 36 (2004) 41–57.

[36] J. Dix, Handbook for Death Scene Investigators, CRC Press LLC, USA, 1999.

[37] W. Castro, Purizaca, La escena del Hecho, Universidad Alas Peruanas, Perú, Monografía, 2006.

[38] Z. Bear, Crime scene responders: the imperative sequential steps, Crit. Care Nurs. Q. (1999) 75–89. May.

[39] M. Soto, P. Nicolas, Biologia Forense, Universidad Internacional de Andalucia, 2005.

[40] Vmer de São Francisco Xavier, descrição, 2007 (revisto em, s.d.) (consultado em 07-06-2007) Disponível em URL: <www.mundo.iol.pt/vmersfx>.

[41] M. Barnes, Preserving Evidence When a Reportable Death Occurs in a Health Care Setting, Coroners Act, October 2003, pp. 208–212.

[42] D.P. Lyle, Forensic for Dummies, Wiley Publishing, Canada, 2004.

[43] S. Moakes, T. Killner, Nurses' understanding of their role as part of a mobile medical and nursing team during a major incident In Pre-Hospital Immediate Care n°5, Birmingham: (s.l.), 2001.

[44] Evidence Collection Guidelines, (consultado em 18-08-2008). Disponivel em <http://www.crime-scene-investigation.net/collect.html>.

[45] L. Flores, Inspeccion tecnico policial (consultado em 12-09-2008). Disponível em www.monografias.com.

[46] M. Health, Scene Assessment: Emergency Treatment Guidelines, August 2003, pp. 3–5.

[47] D. Fried, The Crime Scene and the EMT; Pre-Hospital Trauma. Life Support, 1 (2006) 2–3.

[48] S. County, Medical Professionals at the Scene, ALS Protocols, 2005, pp. 10–23.

[49] B. Long, Lusodidacta Emergências e Catástrofes na Comunidade In Enfermagem Médico-Cirúrgica, 5ª edição, Conceitos e Prática Clínica, Lisboa, 1995.

[50] C. McInerney, Nurses at the crime scene, N. Engl. Ed. 24 (1998) 4–5.

[51] R. Downing, Assessment and Documentation of Strangulation Injuries, IAFN Scientific Assembly, 2007.

[52] L. Cadiou, 250 Fiches Pratiques du Sauveteur en Mission, Éditions Estem, Paris, 2006. ISBN 2-84371-321-8.

[53] M. López, Emergências Médicas, 4ª edição, Guanabara Koogan, Rio de Janeiro, 1984.

[54] T. Harpster, S. Adams, Analyzing 911 Homicide Calls: Practical Aspects and Applications, CRC Press, NW, 2017.

Further reading

B.L. Adams, M.P. Trimble, Nurses in Prehospital Systems and Medical Oversight/National Association of EMS Physicians, Mosby Lifeline, St. Louis, Missouri, 1994.

É. Baccino, Médecine de la Violence, Masson, Paris, 2006.

A. Batuca, Emergências- Suporte básico de vida In Manual de Sinais Vitais, Formasau, Coimbra, 1996.

A. Borges, Centro de Informação Antivenenos (CIAV), INSTITUTO NACIONAL DE EMERGÊNCIA MÉDICA – II Jornadas de Emergência Médica 1980–1990 – Documentação, Expresso Gráfico, Lisboa, 1990. Ministério da Saúde.

J. Braz, Investigação Criminal, Almedina, Coimbra, 2009.

A. Buquet, Manuel de Criminalistique Moderne et de Police Scientifique, 3e Eds., Puf, France, 2006.

M. Byrd, Crime Scene Evidence: A Guide to the Recovery and Collection of Physical Evidence, Staggs Publishing, USA, 2001.

J. Cavellat, J. Chassevent, P. Lecointre, Soins d'Urgence – La Démarche Pratique, Masson, Paris, 2005.

D.W. Clemens, Introduction to crime scene reconstruction, MAFS Newsl. 27 (2) (1998).

F.L. Cole, E. Ramirez, H. Luna-Gonzales, Scope of Practice for the Nurse Practitioner in the Emergency Care Setting, Emergency Nurses Association, Des Plaines, IL, 1999 (revisto em, s.d.). Disponível em URL <www.ena.org>.

Conseil de l'Europe, Étude comparative sur l'organisation et le fonctionnement des services d'aide médicale urgente, Conseil de l'Europe, Strasbourg, 1990.

P.D. Costa, Sistema Integrado de Emergência Médica: Conceção e Perspetivas, INSTITUTO NACIONAL DE EMERGÊNCIA MÉDICA – II Jornadas de Emergência Médica 1980–1990 – Documentação, Expresso Gráfico, Lisboa, 1990. Ministério da Saúde.

J.M.B. Costa, Maddie, Joana e a investigação criminal, 2ª Edição, Livros de Hoje, Lisboa, 2007.

M. Cusson, Criminologia, Casa das Letras, Lisboa, 2002.

V. Di Maio, D. Di Maio, Forensic Pathology, 2nd Edition, CRC Press LLC, USA, 2001.

Direito Mortuário, Lisboa: Dislivro, 2007.

R. Encarnação, Consumo de álcool é a quarta causa de morte (consultado em 16 de Janeiro 2009). Disponível em <http://www.bragancanet.pt/picote/portugues/imprensa/200106/pub_consumo_alcool.htm>.

B. Fisher, Techniques of Crime Scene Investigation, 7th Edition, CRC Press LLC, USA, 2004.

V. Geberth, The staged crime scene, Law Order Mag. 44 (2) (1996) 11–15.

M. Giroud, L'AMU EN FRANCE: Principales Caracteristiques In INSTITUTO NACIONAL DE EMERGÊNCIA MÉDICA – II Jornadas de Emergência Médica 1980–1990 - Documentação, Expresso Gráfico, Lisboa, 1990. Ministério da Saúde.

J. Gomes, Quais os fatores que influenciam o desempenho do enfermeiro enquanto condutor da Viatura Médica de Emergência e Reanimação? Lisboa: Escola Superior de Enfermagem de Calouste Gulbenkian de Lisboa, 2002. Estudo de investigação enquadrado no ano de formação complementar na licenciatura em Enfermagem.

J. Gouveia, VMER: consolidação e alargamento do projeto In INSTITUTO NACIONAL DE EMERGÊNCIA MÉDICA—Via Verde para a Vida: Newsletter do INEM.n°3, Lisboa, 2002.

H. Grant, et al., Emergency Care, Prentice Hall, New Jersey, 1994.

D. Gurchiek, Seven situations in which EMS could become evidence in court, EMS. Rev. (2005) 10–13. January.

J. Henriques, Sistemas de Emergência Médica, INEM, Lisboa, 1983.

J.K. Hensen, Emergency medical services: responses to shootings and stabbings as predictors of homicide, Acad. Emerg. Med. 10 (5) (2003) 536–537.

S. Howarth, A Idade Média, Caminho, Lisboa, 1994.

A. Hoyo, F.E. Galicondo, 2° Curso de Patologia Forense, Universidad del Pais Basco, Facultad de Medicina, San Sebastian, 2001.

Instituto Nacional de Emergência Médica, Manual do serviço de helicópteros de emergência médica, DSM/DSF, Lisboa, 1999.

Instituto Nacional de Emergência Médica, Manual VMER, 2°edição, Ministério da Saúde, Lisboa, 1999.

Instituto Nacional de Emergência Médica, A Estrela da Vida, Símbolo do INEM, 3ªEdição, Instituto Nacional de Emergência Médica, 2001 [consultado em 15-06-2008]. Disponível em URL <www.inem.min-saude.pt>.

Instituto Nacional de Emergência Médica, Centro Rádio Médico – CODU-MAR, 2ºEdição, Instituto Nacional de Emergência Médica e Ministério da Saúde, 2003 [consultado em 15-06-2008]. Disponível em URL <www.inem.min-saude.pt>.

Instituto Nacional de Emergência Médica, Intoxicações, 8°Edição, Instituto Nacional de Emergência Médica e Ministério da Saúde, 2003 [consultado em 15-06-2008]. Disponivel em URL <www.inem.min-saude.pt>.

Instituto Nacional de Emergência Médica, Em caso de emergência ligue 112, n.° Europeu de Socorro, Instituto Nacional de Emergência Médica e Ministério da Saúde, 2004a (consultado em 15-06-2008). Disponível em URL: <www.inem.min-saude.pt>.

J. Laborie, Pathologies Circonstacielles, Réanimation et Urgences Pré-Hospitalières, 4ème Édition, Éditions Frison-Roche, Paris, 2005.

G. Le Boterf, De la Compétence, Les Éditions D'organisations, Paris, 1994.

J. Lincon, O subsistema de transporte do Recém-Nascido em risco: Retrospetiva da sua instalação e funcionamento in INSTITUTO NACIONAL DE EMERGÊNCIA MÉDICA – II Jornadas de Emergência Médica 1980–1990 - Documentação, Expresso Gráfico, Lisboa, 1990. Ministério da Saúde.

G. Ludwig, A must: staging areas for violent crime scenes, emsresponder.com – Firehouse Magazine, 6/11/2008, pp. 1–3.

V. Lynch, Forensic Nursing, Elsevier Mosby, USA, 2006.

F. Marcão, CODU-MAR Medical Advice Centre – Network (MAC-NET PORT), INSTITUTO NACIONAL DE EMERGÊNCIA MÉDICA – II Jornadas de Emergência Médica 1980–1990 - Documentação, Expresso Gráfico, Lisboa, 1990. Ministério da Saúde.

L. McCracken, Guidelines for the Preservation of Physical Evidence in Living Patients, USA, 1998, pp. 2–4.

B. McGyllivray, The Role of Victorian Emergency Nurses in the Collection and Preservation of Forensic Evidence: a Review of the Literature [Em Linha], Medline, USA, 2004 [consulta. Nov. 2007]. Disponível em URL <http://medline.com>.

S. Mittal, S. Gang, Need of clinical forensic medicine in trauma care, 7 (3) (2007-07; 2007-09).

M. Muscari, Forensic Techniques; Advance for Nurses, fev. 2004, pp. 1–4.

W. Patrol, Physical Evidence Handbook; Forensic Laboratory Services Bureau, 2006.

C. Paula, Centro de Orientação de Doentes Urgentes (CODU), INSTITUTO NACIONAL DE EMERGÊNCIA MÉDICA – II Jornadas de Emergência Médica 1980–1990 - Documentação, Expresso Gráfico, Lisboa, 1990. Ministério da Saúde.

G. Peng, Algumas considerações sobre o trabalho de inspeção ao local do crime; Investigação criminal e sistema jurídico, Escola de Polícia Judiciaria, pp. 52–59.

R. Pinto, et al., Emergências e Urgências Médicas Sistema Integrado de Emergência Médica In Revista Referência, n°9, novembro, 2002.

P. Roland, Cenas de Crime, Livro de Hoje, Lisboa, 2007.

R. Saferstein, Criminalistics: An Introduction to Forensic Science, 6th Ed., Prentice Hall, USA, 1998.

L. Sanches, INEM- Via Verde para a comunicação, Instituto Superior de Administração, Comunicação e Empresa, Lisboa, 2003.

Scene Assessment, (consultado em 12-11-2007). Disponivel em <www.hopperinstitute.com/emt_scene.html>.

G. Schiro, Collection and preservation of blood evidence from crime scene, J. Forensic Identif. 20 (2) (1997).

E. Silva, Verificação da morte: remoção de corpos da via publica; Parecer N° 1/NAT/2000; 28/02/2000.

F. Silva, P. Costa, T. Gonçalves, Emergência médica em Portugal: um longo caminho que conheceu já etapas decisivas In Emergência Médica, Instituto nacional de Emergência Médica, Lisboa, 1987.

W.U. Spitz, Medicolegal Investigation of Death, 4th Edition, Charles C. Thomas Publisher, USA, 2004.

C. Thomas, Dicionário médico enciclopédico Taber, 17ª ed., Lusodidacta, Loures, 2000.

J. Tintinalli, E. Ruiz, R. Krome, Emergências Médicas, 4ª Ed., Guanabara, México, 1996.

U.S. Department of Justice, A Guide for Law Enforcement, Office of Justice Programs, Washington, 1999.

U.S. Department of Justice, Federal Bureau of Investigation Laboratory Division: Handbook of Forensic Services, Virginia, 2003.

A. Ventura, Opinião, Urgência/Emergência e INEM In Instituto Nacional de Emergência Médica—Via Verde para a Vida: Newsletter do INEM. n°3, Lisboa, 2002. ISSN: 1645–3751.

M. Wong, Estudo autópsico de las muertes violentas, 2005 (consultado em 20-10-2008). Disponivel em. <www.conganat.org/7congress/final/vistaimpression.asp?id_trabajo = 173>.